CONTENTS

ACKNOWLEDGMENTS

This study has gained from the participation of friends and colleagues. First my thanks to Nicholas Stargardt and Anthony Smith of Magdalen College, Oxford, for hosting the presentation of the central chapters of this book in a series of lectures in that congenial and stimulating place; to Maria Tatar for commenting on the theoretical thrust of the opening chapter; to Willem de Blécourt for reading the Grimm chapter and making the Wild girls the right age; to Lewis Seifert for an insightful reading of the French chapter; to Suzanne Magnanini for opening my eyes to that strangely tantalizing world of Neapolitan Baroque literature; to Nancy Canepa for lending her expertise in Basile scholarship; and to the international journal of folk narrative research, *Fabula*, for its permission to incorporate portions of my article, "Fairy Tale Origins, Fairy Tale Dissemination, and Folk Narrative Theory" into chapters 1 and 5; to Karl Bottigheimer, always my first reader; to SUNY Press's anonymous readers for suggesting points to clarify and expand; and finally to members of the Stony Brook Interlibrary Loan office, who year after year make this kind of research possible, with special thanks to Donna Sammis for constant support.

ONE

WHY A NEW HISTORY
OF FAIRY TALES?

INTRODUCTION

Most traditional histories of fairy tales begin with an unlettered country folk that invents fairy tales and then passes them along by word of mouth from generation to generation. Somewhat less frequently, fairy tales have been presented as disintegrations of ancient myth, as the remains of paleolithic beliefs, as fictionalized remnants of elementary planetary observations, or as evidence of universal archetypes. Such explanations have resulted in a sense that fairy tales' origins are elusive, a sense of elusiveness that has shaped grand narratives of the genre as well as references to fairy tales in books about history, literature (including children's literature), psychology, and folklore. It has been said so often that the folk invented and disseminated fairy tales that this assumption has become an unquestioned proposition. It may therefore surprise readers that folk invention and transmission of fairy tales has no basis in verifiable fact. Literary analysis undermines it, literary history rejects it, social history repudiates it, and publishing history (whether of manuscripts or of books) contradicts it.

The current understanding of the history of fairy tales is not only built on a flimsy foundation; its very basis requires an absence of evidence. A belief in fairy tales' oral origins requires that there be no written records of fairy tales themselves. This perception goes against the grain of every scholarly undertaking since the scientific revolution made evidence the central plank of its platform.

People who subscribe to a belief in fairy tales' oral origins and dissemination are not embarrassed by the fact that all references to old women or other people's telling tales or stories before 1550 are just that—references to old women or other people telling *stories*, and the most we learn about the stories themselves is that some of them had witches or monsters. Inadequate to prove that fairy tales existed in the ancient and medieval worlds, those reports merely validate the existence of storytelling in the ancient world, a fact that has, however, never been in doubt.

Anyone living in a structure with a foundation as rickety as the edifice that houses the traditional study of fairy tales would search out strong timbers to prop it up. In recent years that has indeed happened but with problematic results. In *The Uses of Enchantment* Bruno Bettelheim implies that as children's psyches develop, their changing psychological needs result in their projecting complementarily constructed fairy tale plots to provide solace for and understanding of their own young lives and experiences. A tension runs throughout Bettelheim's book between the fact of the fairy tales' book sources and an implication that children and their psychological needs authored fairy tales' plots, although he never explicitly deals with that issue. His views, although initially persuasive, have not weathered close scrutiny. Jack Zipes's effort to shore up the weak structure of fairy tales' origins and history in *Why Fairy Tales Stick* takes a different tack: he attributes fairy tales' remarkable staying power to brain modules, for which he has borrowed the term "memes." Bettelheim and Zipes are the best known of many fairy tale scholars in the United States, England, France, and Germany who have incorporated folk creation and dissemination into their theoretical structure of fairy tales' origins and history. Along with making valuable contributions to the study of fairy tales, these many scholars have accepted theories of long standing in the secondary literature about fairy tales in good faith. *Fairy Tales: A New History* will offer evidence and reasons for an alternative history.

It is difficult to question long-held beliefs, such as the belief that the folk invented and then communicated fairy tales from one generation to the next, from one country to another, and from language to language. These are long-accepted, hallowed beliefs, and so I won't ask readers to accept a new proposition without strong evidence of its own. Instead, I invite them to make a journey of exploration, examination, and discovery along with me.

Thinking about fairy tales begins by thinking about the differences between folk tales and fairy tales. Fairy tales are often called "folk tales" in the belief that unlettered folk storytellers created both kinds of stories. But treating fairy tales and folk tales as one and the same thing obscures fundamental, and significant, differences between them.

LITERARY ANALYSIS

Folk Tales

In their terminologies, traditional histories of fairy tales generally conflate two terms, "fairy tale" and "folk tale." Interchanging the two terms leads to terminological misunderstandings and results in confounding difficulties for any discussion of fairy and folk tales. It's therefore necessary to distinguish clearly between folk tales and fairy tales and to clarify their differing histories and separate identities.

Folk tales differ from fairy tales in their structure, their cast of characters, their plot trajectories, and their age. Brief, and with linear plots, folk tales reflect the world and the belief systems of their audiences.[1] Taking their characters from that familiar world, folk tales are typically peopled with husbands and wives, peasants, thieving rascals, or an occasional doctor, lawyer, priest, or preacher. In a typical folk tale plot, one person makes off with another person's money, goods, or honor. More to the point, a very large proportion of folk tales *don't* have a happy ending. Marital strife looms large, because typical folk tales that include a married couple are not about the joys of *getting* married, but about the difficulties of *being* married.

Folk tales are easy to follow and easy to remember, in part because they deal with familiar aspects of the human condition, like the propensity to build castles in the air. Take, for example, the ancient tale of a peasant who had a jug of honey and who dreamed of selling it profitably and being able to buy a flock of chickens. He imagined he'd earn enough from selling the resulting eggs to buy a piglet. When it grew up, it would bear piglets of its own that he could sell for even more money. As is typical for a folk tale, the peasant expected his profits to mount steadily so that he could eventually buy a goat—or a sheep—or a cow. Finally, the daydreaming peasant imagined that he'd build a house, marry, and have a son, whom—in his reverie—he imagined he'd beat when he misbehaved. Flailing about him, the peasant smashed the precious honey jug—and with that, he destroyed his dreams of wealth. Such an ending typifies many folk tales[2] and has long existed, at least since it was documented nearly 1500 years ago in the Indian *Panchatantra*. The story's wry acceptance of sad consequences and limited possibilities for its poor hero fit it into a category of anecdotal and joke folk tales classified as ATU 1430. There are even folktales in which a swineherd marries a princess or in which a goosegirl marries a prince, as in Tale Types 850 and 870, but on close examination these apparently fairy tale endings have no magic about them.

Instead, their unexpected weddings come about through poor folks' cunning, and they are thus categorized as "realistic tales." Even a few tales routinely called "fairy tales," such as Perrault's "Three Wishes" (ATU 750), are by common consent categorized as "religious tales" in the Aarne-Thompson-Uther classification.

Tales of Magic

As a category, tales of magic necessarily include magic. Magic exists across a broad spectrum of tales, some of which are fairy tales and many of which are not. For instance, an anecdote about an individual who experiences an uncanny and unsettling encounter with one or more extranatural creatures is often an urban legend, while a tale in which a god or goddess magically transforms a human being into something else (such as a tree or a cow or a star) is generally termed a legend. Tales in the Judaeo-Christian community in which saints, angels, or God himself intervene in the lives of human beings are religious tales. In these examples the fantastic, the divine, the magical, the miraculous, and the transformative produce examples of awe of the other-worldly, examples of divine power and divine truth rather than the wedding, earthly happiness, and well-being associated with fairy tales.

The Aarne-Thompson-Uther tale-type classification groups a broad variety of tales together as "Tales of Magic." Some verge on wisdom tales, like one that describes a contest between the sun and the wind to see which can make a traveler take off his coat. When the wind blows as hard as it can, the traveller holds his coat more tightly about him. But when the sun shines gently, he takes it off. Others are exotic oriental tales steered by magic, like ones from *Thousand and One Nights*, in which a magic rug might carry an individual from one continent to another in a matter of seconds, or in which a wicked princess might magically turn her opponents into stone.

Among tales of magic are ones more familiar to readers of fairy tales. In many of them, a youth kills a dragon, thereby rescuing a princess whom he subsequently marries. Sometimes the bold youth is a prince; sometimes he's the youngest and most virtuous brother in a family of starving peasants (or shoemakers or swineherds or woodcutters). Rescuing princesses from all sorts of dangers and all sorts of places and then marrying them ranks high among tales of magic. Traditionally, princesses who rescue princes are relatively rare, although not entirely unknown. More familiar are poor girls who with the considerable help of magic marry princes and in the process have to contend with one or more jealous girls and women: sisters, stepsisters, stepmothers, witches, or mothers-in-law. The tales of magic that end in weddings all share the welcome ending of two people's difficulties and the beginning of a life lived happily ever after. Common usage and scholarly terminology both recognize these tales as fairy tales.

Fairy Tales: "Oral" and "Literary"

We have now separated fairy tales out from folk tales and general tales of magic, but there remains one other theoretical distinction, one that is highly problematic. The widespread belief that an unlettered folk created fairy tales has led to the category of *folk* fairy tales. Sometimes other names are used: *real* fairy tales, *pure* fairy tales, *genuine* fairy tales, or *uncontaminated* fairy tales. Each of these words implies that fairy tales were created within an oral ("pure" or "genuine") culture and were transmitted through oral cultures as "folk fairy tales" until they were written down by later authors, who collected them from the folk (but "contaminated" them in so doing). Phrases like "write down" and "collect" strongly suggest an act of appropriation, as Marxist critics would express it, a kind of intellectual piracy or theft from an unlettered teller by a literate author. Scholars' utilization of words like "pure" and "uncontaminated" implies, without actually stating, adherence to a traditional history of orally composed and disseminated fairy tales. Since the general public widely believes in fairy tales' oral composition and transmission, those phrases buy a certain credibility for writers who use them. At the same time, using a vocabulary of implied oralism further authorizes the traditional history, because it appears to accept that history, without having to certify a position vis-à-vis the entire proposition of fairy tales' possible relationships to oral or literate culture. In the end, using language such as "writing down" a fairy tale avoids dealing with central issues concerning paradigms of orality or literacy within which fairy tales might be analyzed.

The term "literary fairy tale" has come to be understood as a reworking of orally composed and transmitted tales. In this context, "reworking" is understood to have been carried out by literate, and literary, authors like Giovan Francesco Straparola, Giambattista Basile, Marie-Catherine d'Aulnoy, Charles Perrault, Jacob and Wilhelm Grimm, and by many other writers whose names and collections will be named later. In the case of the Grimms, it was long—and erroneously—believed that they had made great efforts to preserve existing, but nearly extinct, folk versions of the tales published in their collection, whereas in fact their fifty years of editing can be fairly characterized as having turned widely available tales from literary sources into carefully crafted reflections of contemporary folk grammatical usage and contemporary bourgeois beliefs about folk social values. (Whether they did so consciously or unconsciously is another matter altogether.)

Simply using the term "literary" fairy tale powerfully implies an existence of another sort of fairy tale, an oral sort. The historical analysis of chapters 2, 3, and 4 will show that the existence of oral fairy tales, as they are defined above and will be further defined below, among *any* folk before the nineteenth century cannot be demonstrated. The terms "oral" and "literary" usefully distinguish between literary styles in fairy tales. But in terms of the history of fairy tales, terms like "oral" and "literary" inaccurately and misleadingly suggest that a set of distinctions exist that cannot be proven to have existed before the nineteenth century. Their use serves only to advance an unproveable theory of oral origins and transmission, and I'll therefore avoid them in what follows.

Fairy Tales

So far the discussion has not led to a usable working definition of fairy tales, and that is the subject now at hand. "Fairy tale" is a much misunderstood term, and the source for the confusion about the nature of "fairy tales" is the title of a single book, *Grimm's Fairy Tales*. The book's original title, *Kinder- und Haus-märchen* (Nursery and Household Tales), had no fairies in its brief wording, a logically reasonable reflection of the fact that so few fairies can be found in the tales themselves. The contents of the book, *Grimm's Fairy Tales*, offers instead a mixed lot of animal tales; tales of origins that explain, for instance, why the moon hangs in the sky; warning tales, among which is the famous "Red Riding Hood" that tells little girls to stay on the path and not talk to strangers; and folk tales whose characters usually end up where they started, like the starveling fisherman and his wife who briefly had an emperor's palace before they were plunged back into wretched poverty. There are even religious tales like "Mary's Child" that pitch their heroines into suffering and threaten even greater pain if they don't tell the truth.[3]

The Aarne-Thompson-Uther *Types of International Folktales* avoids the term "fairy tale" altogether, instead designating Tale Types 300–749 as "Tales of Magic." In the "Introduction" to the *Oxford Companion to Fairy Tales*, Jack Zipes cites miraculous transformations, a happy ending, the presence of stock characters, settings, and motifs as determining components of "oral" wonder tales. According to Zipes, "writing [them] down" resulted in "literary" fairy tales (xvii–xix). Writing about folktales in

Donald Haase's *Greenwood Encyclopedia of Folktales and Fairy Tales*, Maria Nikolajeva takes a cautiously print culture stance in noting that folktales are "a form of traditional, fictional, prose narrative that is said to circulate orally" (363), while Donald Haase accepts a distinction between "folktale" and "literary fairy tale" and provides a history and description of several scholars' attempts to define the term, but takes no position vis-à-vis those definitions there (322).

Most definitions of fairy tales center on the tales' structure and component motifs. In *Fairy Tales: A New History*, however, I'll view fairy tales as *narratives* whose plot, that is, whose narrative trajectory, is a fundamentally defining part of their very being. I accept the central importance of fairy tale motifs, fairy tale structure, and fairy tale happy endings, but none of those categories, in and of themselves, achieves a workable definition for fairy tales. Fairy tale motifs such as magic rings and the number three appear in fifteenth- and sixteenth-century Italian romances; fairy tale structure, Proppian or otherwise, underlies a great many novels; and fairy tale happy endings define nineteenth-, twentieth-, and twenty-first-century bodice-ripping romances. Thus it is not motifs, structure, or happy endings alone that define fairy tales, but the overall plot trajectory of individual tales in conjunction with those fairy tale elements all brought together within a "compact" narrative, to borrow a term from Elizabeth Harries's *Twice Upon a Time* (16–17). All this together creates a fairy tale as we know it in the modern world and as it first appeared in the sixteenth century.

Length, too, is central to defining fairy tales. After all, some lengthy medieval romances, predating by hundreds of years fairy tales as we now know them, built in all the elements (motifs, structure, happy ending) of modern fairy tales. But their interminable length separates them incontrovertibly from the genre of fairy tales. In the age of print, books prepared for a popular market were routinely abbreviated, and when they appeared in drastically shortened form with their conclusions more often happy than unhappy, they emerged from a long medieval history into the world of early modern print as something that began to resemble modern fairy tales.

Restoration Fairy Tales

Restoration fairy tales are firmly based in the world of human beings.[4] Like their medieval precursors, they begin with a royal personage—usually a prince or princess, but sometimes a king or queen—who is driven away from home and heritage. Out in the world, the royals face adventures, undertake tasks, and suffer hardships and trials. With magic assistance they succeed in carrying out their assigned tasks, overcoming their imposed hardships, and enduring their character-testing trials, after which they marry royally and are restored to a throne, that is, they return to their just social, economic, and political position. The Grimms' "Twelve Brothers" (Zwölf Brüder) is a classic restoration tale:

> A royal pair had twelve sons, but the king vowed that if the next child were a daughter, the boys should be killed and their inheritance given to the girl (sic). When a girl was in fact born, the brothers fled. Some years later, the princess learned of her brothers and set off in search of them. Having accidentally turned them into ravens, she suffered seven years' silence to redeem them. Although she nearly died from the hardships of her long trial, in the end she married a king and lived happily ever after.

Classic authors of fairy tales in the sixteenth, seventeenth, and eighteenth centuries—Straparola in Venice, Basile in Naples, Perrault and d'Aulnoy in Paris, Leprince de Beaumont in London—all composed restoration fairy tales, although they did so with considerable variation. For instance, the well known restoration fairy tale "Sleeping Beauty" has a heroine who does little to bring about her return to royal station. In its Basilean,

Perrauldian, and Grimm incarnations, the heroine remains pas-
sive, her sole adventure a century-long sleep, after which a
prince who providentially arrives, weds her, and thus restores her
to her just royal station.

```
   royal origins *                    * royal restoration
                 \                    /
                  \                  /
                   \                /
                    \              /
                     \            /
                      ^^^^^^^^^^ (tasks, tests, trials, and sufferings)
```

If charted visually, restoration fairy tales start high, fall low,
and then return to their original social level. The hardships of
suffering royalty (^^^^^) are narratively extensible, and, as was
the case in the medieval romances that preceded restoration
fairy tales, heroes' and heroines' adventures, tasks, tests, trials,
and sufferings could be, and sometimes seem to have been,
extended endlessly. In contrast, classic restoration *fairy* tales generally trimmed the test-task-trial part of the story to three
episodes, more or less.

Straparola's inclusion of restoration fairy tales in his collection established their abbreviated fairy-tale length in a published
prose form. Even so, Straparola's restoration fairy tales remained
significantly longer than a second kind of fairy tale in his collection, whose cast of characters began with, and was sometimes
dominated by, poor people. The greater length that Straparola
accorded his restoration fairy tales generally continued to characterize the stories about royal heroes and heroines in subsequent
restoration fairy tales well into the nineteenth century.

Rise Fairy Tales

Rise fairy tales begin with a dirt-poor girl or boy who suffers the
effects of grinding poverty and whose story continues with tests,

tasks, and trials until magic brings about a marriage to royalty and a happy accession to great wealth.[5] The earliest enduringly popular rise fairy tale is Straparola's "Puss in Boots," in which a youngest son, left penniless at his mother's death, is helped by a fairy cat to marriage with a princess and consequently to great wealth. The plot has remained popular to the present day as a fairy tale and in a number of other genres.

A rise fairy tale is occasionally extended by the addition of a lengthening coda, a practice for which the Grimms' "Rumpelstiltskin" provides a good example. There a poor girl's rise to queenship is complicated by the bargain she made with a magical creature who had helped her achieve her royal marriage. Working out the secondary plot temporarily retards the achievement of the tale's ultimately happy ending:

> There was once a miller who told the king his daughter could spin straw to gold. The king declared that he would marry the girl if she did so, but would have her killed if she didn't. Brought into a chamber filled with straw, the girl despaired, but a gnome appeared and magically performed the impossible task, for which she rewarded him with her neckerchief. When he helped her a second time she gave him her ring, but on the third occasion, having nothing left to give, she promised her firstborn child.
>
> The king married her, and some time later the girl, now a queen, gave birth to a beautiful baby. Shortly afterward the gnome arrived to claim his reward, and when she protested, he said he'd relent if she could guess his name. On the third try, the queen said, "Rumpelstiltskin," was released from her promise, and lived happily ever after.

Straparola's rise tales were generally shorter than his restoration tales, and the shorter length of rise tales remained one of their features in the following centuries. Their plot trajectory can be charted visually: a rise tale begins with a poor and lowly hero or heroine who rises dramatically up the social ladder. The rise fairy tale plot became so popular in the early 1800s that it eventually led to rewritings of some restoration fairy tale plots to make them fit the rise fairy tale model. "Cinderella," for instance, is generally understood to be a rise fairy tale in which a poor girl gets a prince. However, in its first appearance in the 1630s, the heroine was not poor at all, but a prince's daughter who had one tormenting stepmother after another, until she was magically helped to a royal ball, where she found a princely husband and a return to a life of ease and comfort.

Fairy tales continue to resonate in people's lives. This is largely so because fairy tales originated among the same kinds of urban assumptions and expectations with which city and suburban dwellers continue to live today. Fairy tales, which speak in a language well understood in the modern world, remain relevant because they allude to deep hopes for material improvement, because they present illusions of happiness to come, and because they provide social paradigms that overlap nearly perfectly with daydreams of a better life.

This brief literary analysis demonstrates that folk tales and fairy tales differ fundamentally from one another in their narrative trajectories. The two kinds of stories also appear to offer different kinds of storytelling for different sorts of audiences. At this point, it is not possible to declare more precisely what constitutes the audiences' conjectured differences, and so let us continue by refining a definition of fairy tales in an expanded context.

LITERARY HISTORY

Fairies vs. Tales about Fairies and Fairyland

The questions addresssed here are twofold: Are fairies an integral part of fairy tales? If so, does the presence of fairies or fairyland in a tale make that tale a fairy tale?

The British Isles have an extraordinarily rich fairy lore. Well into the eighteenth century, ordinary folks used the fairy universe of extranaturals to make sense of otherwise inexplicable processes and events. Wilkies (who were connected with the dead) had to be propitiated. Brownies (who attached themselves to particular people) had to be appreciated for the good they did around the house, though they mustn't be personally acknowledged or thanked. Fairies could carry off a beautiful infant and substitute a malformed changeling. Wilkies, brownies, fairies, and scores of other little people[6] accounted for the incomprehensibility of unexpected deaths, misshapen infants, dry udders, and missing clothes.

In their childrearing and childcare parents and servants invoked supernatural creatures (of the sort that were known to kidnap and eat little boys and girls) in order to frighten children into docile obedience. One result was that educational reformers like Francis Bacon and John Locke in England and pedagogical theorists like Joachim Campe in Germany inveighed against ignorant servants who used goblins and ghosts to control the young people in their care.[7] Extranaturals were most often to be found in chapbooks for the poor,[8] but some—like Robin Goodfellow and Queen Mab—found their way into high literature like Shakespeare's *Midsummer Night's Dream* as well as into operas and masques.

Tales about Fairies and Fairyland

Edmund Spenser's *Faerie Queene* (1590) and Ben Jonson's *Oberon, The Faery Prince: A Masque of Prince Henries* (the masque was presented in 1611 and printed in 1616) expanded fairy literature to include much more about the world that fairies inhabited, and they can therefore be said to be tales about fairyland.[9] The same was true of Michael Drayton's *Nymphidia* (1627). Fairies were all the rage in the early 1600s, and these three are only a tiny fraction of many private and public high culture fairy and fairyland appearances.[10] In England, fairy poetry such as Spenser's, Jonson's, and Drayton's had by and large ended by 1650,[11] but it lived on at the French court of Versailles.

In general, early—that is, medieval or early modern—tales about fairyland are built on a strong Celtic underlay onto which English, French, German, and Italian authors grafted large amounts of indigenous fairy belief. The most significant aspect of tales about fairyland, however, is that they depict two parallel worlds, a fairy universe and the human world. The human worlds in tales about fairyland are more or less familiar with the exception of occasional encounters with fairies, with people being born, living happy or unhappy lives, and dying. The fairy universe, on the other hand, differs dramatically from the human world. Subject to different natural laws, fairyland time is often decelerated, so that one year there equals multiple, sometimes a hundred, years in the human world. The consequences of such differences for mortal visitors can be, and often are, disastrous. Even if humans' visits to fairyland have seemed brief, their absence from the human world has been far longer than they believed to be the case, and as a result, visitors returning home from fairyland find their own world changed beyond recognition. (Washington Irving's Rip van Winkle experienced a nineteenth-century version of this fairyland condition.[12]) Even worse, fairyland's retarded passage of time holds normal physiological aging at bay, so that people who return to the human world from a fairyland visit of only a few days, weeks, or months suddenly shrivel, wrinkle, and die as their mortal bodies, no longer protected against aging by fairyland's slowed time, catch up with the mortal passage of time.[13]

In the later 1600s, tales about fairyland diminished in importance among England's upper classes, but survived and persisted for another hundred years as a set of beliefs held by and published for country people and uneducated but literate city dwellers. In the same period in France, tales about fairyland continued as a literary idyll among the French aristocracy. One person who left a record of the fashionable fairy fad was the noblewoman Madame de Sévigné (1626–1696). Corresponding with her daughter from the royal court at Versailles on August 6, 1677, Madame de Sévigné wrote that court ladies had amused themselves for nearly an hour by listening to a story about a princess who was reared on earth before a fairy lover carried her off to fairyland in a crystal coach. Madame de Sévigné reported that the ladies called this activity "mitonner."[14]

Nobody wrote down this kind of oral chit-chat until the Countess d'Aulnoy (1650/51–1705) did so in 1690. In that year, she composed a long novel, *Histoire d'Hipolyte, comte de Duglas* (The Story of Hypolitus, Count of Douglas). Into this lengthy novel she introduced a tale about a fairyland called "The Isle of Happiness" (L'Île de Félicité). Its plot went roughly this way:

A human hero joined his beloved, a fairy queen, in fairyland. After a year there he wished to visit his homeland. She granted him permission to do so, but warned him to remain on his fairyland horse. [The horse represented a protective equine extension of fairyland's protective powers into the hero's mortal world.] But tricked into dismounting, he was overtaken by death.

Madame d'Aulnoy soon wrote another tale about fairyland, "The Yellow Dwarf" (Le Nain jaune). There a hateful dwarf kills the handsome King of the Golden Mountain; the king's beloved, a princess, falls dead upon his chest; and together their unending love turns them into palm trees that eternally incline towards one another.

The distinguishing characteristics of tales about fairyland—two parallel universes and sometimes unhappy endings—make their differentness from fairy tales obvious. Despite these fundamental differences in location and outcome, tales about fairyland are often, and confusingly, lumped together with human-centered and real-world-based fairy tales.[15] The existence of tales about fairyland in the environs of the French royal court in the 1650s, such as those reported by Madame de Sévigné, and in Paris in the 1690s, is irrelevant to the question of whether fairy tales were present at the French court in the 1650s, because tales about fairyland and fairy tales are two very different kinds of stories (the first might have an unhappy ending, the second always has a happy ending) with very different centers of gravity (one including fairyland, the other in a world inhabited principally by human beings). It would, of course, have been historically possible for restoration and rise fairy tales from Straparola's *Pleasant Nights* to have been present at the French royal court in the 1650s, because all of his tales were physically available in French translation in the 1650s, as the section on publishing history below will show. But the fact is, that there was never a single report of tellings of Straparola's tales at the French court, only Mme de Sévigné's account of *mitonner*, of telling tales about fairies and fairyland, of which no examples existed in Straparola's much-printed book.

SOCIAL HISTORY

In now-famous studies like Emmanuel Le Roy Ladurie's *Montaillou* (1975) and Carlo Ginzburg's *The Cheese and the Worms* (1975) social historians investigated the living conditions of humble folk, looking long and hard at the historical reality of their life in the late medieval and early modern period. Doing so cast a revealing light on differences between the life experiences of poor people living in the country and those living in towns and cities.[16] What such books disclose also makes the proposition that unlettered country folk composed fairy tales seem very unlikely.

Life in the early modern countryside, that is from the early 1500s to the late 1700s, was rigidly organized and tightly controlled. With unceasing toil, a long life, and unending luck, an ambitious peasant boy might add two or three additional hectares of land to his family's holdings. If such good fortune continued over several generations, one of his great- or great-great-grandsons might become a rich enough peasant to aspire to marry a merchant's daughter. That snail-slow chain of events, with its inevitable reverses and temporary setbacks, is consistent with *folk* tale content as described on pages 3–5. A girl in the country, for her part, might be raped by a count or a baron and, in recompense for lost virginity, receive a dowry big enough to assure her of a decent match with a fellow chosen from among her country peers. That's also the stuff of folk tales, where stories shine the hard light of reality onto the poverty-stalked lives of their heros and heroines.[17] It thus seems a realistic assumption that country folk might have invented folk tales of the sort discussed above, but not that they would have conceived of fairy tales, the earliest of which are firmly embedded in the imagery, characters, and references of *city* life.[18]

Boys and girls born and reared in Italian country villages and towns didn't necessarily stay at home, particularly during the Renaissance. The island republic of Venice was one city that attracted young people leaving towns and villages behind them to seek their fortune in Italy's old established metropolitan centers—Rome, Naples, Bologna, Milan, and Venice—or in small but wealthy centers of court culture, like Ferrara and Mantua.

City life differed from country life in primary respects. First, there was a city's relatively large population of thousands of individuals. A typical urban mix included hundreds of servants and more hundreds of artisans and urban workers along with a privileged elite that often included a free-spending urban nobility.

The countryside and cities differed substantially in what constituted wealth. For countrydwellers, it was mainly land that was critical to amassing riches, either in terms of the potential for growing crops and selling the resulting harvest or in terms of sheer ownership, which made it possible to rent out lands you didn't farm yourself. In cities, however, people could wash off most of the mud of country living, while ordinary people might even accumulate money and rise in socio-economic terms. In cities, unlike the country, it was money itself (what you could buy with it and what you could invest in with it) that was the beginning point for amassing riches.

In northern Italy where Venice lay, a high proportion of Renaissance men and women as well as girls and boys were literate,[19] a far higher proportion than was the case among village dwellers. Every town had one or more schools to teach reading and arithmetic to its young boys and a good number of its girls.[20]

The first flush of printing in the mid-1400s had been devoted to manufacturing books for which there was a preexisting demand, the kinds of books that *scriptoria* had been producing for pupils, students, and scholars. Within a generation, however, Renaissance printing presses had begun to turn out books and pamphlets that a broader buyership wanted for its leisure reading. Concurrently an ingrained habit of communicating values by telling stories had survived from the middle ages into the Renaissance. Consequently, priests told stories from the pulpit and on occasion might augment church-provided manuals with tales from the marketplace.[21] Merchants carried amusing little *vademecums* on their travels, some of which consisted almost entirely of folk tales and urban tales of rascality and trickery for bookbuyers both rich and poor.

Because city merchants could, and sometimes did, buy the same books that servants and artisans purchased,[22] the entire range of literate city dwellers was envisaged as a reading public for whom new kinds of tales might be created in Renaissance Venice.[23] As a result, maximizing the sales of any given tale collection assembled in this period meant designing that collection to address a broad potential readership. That, in turn, meant incorporating a variety of life situations into its stories.

Venice in the middle of the sixteenth century was a huge entrepôt. Its international printing industry served a large local bookbuying market as well as distant markets like Naples in southern Italy and, on the other side of the Alps, Lyons in south-central France. In the very period in which Straparola was writing, however, Venice had suffered an economic downturn. Fewer artisans were able to accumulate capital, no matter how hard they worked. Not only that, changing markets, shifting sources of supply, and cheaper goods from abroad were undermining the local economy and destabilizing employment.[24] In these conditions, economic uncertainty stared workers in the face, and they would have known that hard work alone wouldn't lead to prosperity. This was a mental environment that would have been receptive to a new kind of story line, one in which magic facilitated a poor person's ascent to wealth. This was also the age in which stories that we can identify as rise fairy tales first appear.

The elements that make up the fairy tale genre were all in place before the 1550s: the hallmarks of fairy tales—magic objects and sudden acquisitions of wealth—were not new in themselves. What was different was that rise fairy tales built in the kinds of generalized hopes for an improvement in their lives specific to the burgeoning populations of upward-striving young men and women in early modern cities. Since urban money economies entail wealth in coin and cash, it's reasonable to assume that urban hopes of literate but poor readers included dreams of getting rich. But how was that to happen?

In the fairy tales about poor boys and girls getting rich that appeared in Venice in the 1550s, the details are specific to that place—Venice—and to conditions at that time. These brief tales were the first ones in the European tradition in which a poor person, with the help of magic, married a noble or even a member of a royal family and got rich as a result. (See below for an elaboration on this statement.) From the point of view of a poor Venetian boy or girl, such a marriage would have meant a happily-ever-after future with no backbreaking labor, lots of spendable money, and plenty to eat for the rest of their lives. The sticking point, however, was that laws that had been on the

Venetian books since the 1520s forbade marriages between Venice's nobility and its commoners.[25]

It is the intersection of a specific impossibility in real life and its achievement in fantasy that marks the birth of the modern rise fairy tale. Real-world Venetian laws prevented a commoner from marrying nobility, but the forces of supernatural fantasy achieved that goal in a handful of stories that appeared in Giovan Francesco Straparola's *Pleasant Nights*. Socially unequal marriages like this *had* taken place in one or two medieval religious legends, but the motivation for those stories was a desire to show that if God willed it, even an outright impossibility—such as a poor commoner marrying royalty—could be brought about through divine intervention. Straparola's plot line, however, eschewed religious miracles and turned, instead to secular magic to bring a poor girl or boy together with a royal spouse.

The difficulties of achieving a union between a noble and a commoner were compounded in Straparola's Venice, because in addition to being *improbable*, it was also *illegal*. Thus, in his new rise fairy tales Straparola wedded his socially unequal lovers to each other not in Venice but in a distant realm.

Wealth, happiness ever after, and a crown epitomized Venice's fairy tale creations. Of these three happily-ever-after components, the most important was wealth, a fact that Straparola made explicitly clear either in the beginning, middle, or ending of his rise fairy tales.[26] His groundbreaking equation for his fairy tale was:

poverty *through* magic *leads to* marriage *and then* money.

The economic conditions and the legal constraints of Renaissance Venice provided the impossible conditions that Straparola reformulated to give the modern rise fairy tale its particular form. In his new storyline, he transformed a Venetian impossibility into a fairy tale reality. Social history and literary genres exist in an intimate relationship with each other in every age. Renaissance Venice provides an excellent example of the birth of a new genre, the rise fairy tale, in direct response to educational, social, economic, and legal forces.

PUBLISHING HISTORY

From the 1450s onward printing presses became an important part of urban life.[27] This has already been alluded to above in discussing the availability of books in northern Italy in the late 1400s and early 1500s. When printers began to publish for a broad public, they adapted existing manuscript texts such as medieval romances. With their moveable type, printing presses were perfect for producing printed materials that could be edited to suit different sorts of audiences. For leisured listening and reading, they printed long books; for people like artisans and shopkeepers who had less time to spare, they printed short ones, sometimes just a single large sheet folded into 8, 12, 16, or 24 pages. (It could be folded into even more, and smaller, pages, but that happened only seldom in Venice in these years.) Consequently, by the 1470s lots of cheap broadsides and low-priced pamphlets were available for urban readers of modest means. Furthermore, the fact that almost all books were sold unbound, that is, without the added cost of an expensive binding, meant that even some large books were nearly as accessible to the poor as they were to the rich. The rich had their books covered with expensively tooled leather; the poor sewed theirs together at home.

The collection that included Straparola's new plotline, the *Pleasant Nights*, sold well, both in Italy and—in French translation—in France.[28] The plot of his tales of magical social rise ultimately became enormously popular in the modern world, and by the nineteenth and twentieth centuries rise fairy tales dominated the popular market in fairy tales.

The publishing history of fairy tales, both restoration and rise, shows that they were born in Venice in the mid-sixteenth century, were added to in Naples in the early seventeenth century, were developed in France in the late seventeenth century, and were exported to Germany in the second half of the eighteenth century. In the late eighteenth century they began a triumphal march on little book feet throughout literate Europe.[29] In the nineteenth century, school readers spread fairy tales to city and country children alike in Germany[30] and France, and research in progress suggests that similar school readers spread the same tales to British, French, Italian, and German colonies in Africa, Asia, and the New World. In today's world fairy tales are ever-present in young children's books. Publishing history thus provides a paradigm for understanding how fairy tales were distributed to even the remotest corners of every European nation—and beyond—from the 1550s to the present.[31] Publishing history also makes it possible to bridge a divide between public commercial distribution of a set of plots and images on the one hand and the private and personal awareness of those same plots and images on the other hand. For example, many adults have absorbed fairy tales so completely that a small shoe reminds them of the entire "Cinderella" plot, and a thornily ringed castle evokes memories of "Sleeping Beauty."

Scholars have long been puzzled about how "Cinderella," "Sleeping Beauty," and other fairy tales in terms such as this: How did fairy tales pass from one person to another until nineteenth- and twentieth-century folklorists hearkened to peasants' words and wrote them down. For two hundred years, most were satisfied to credit national folks with having invented fairy tales and then having passed them along. In the absence of hard evidence about fairy tales' initial appearance and their movement from one country to another, positing an unlettered folk as fairy tale inventor was an intellectually responsible hypothesis. It was a model that interpreted the absence of historical or documentary evidence that fairy tales existed before the 1550s as proof that their prior existence was—and must have been—in an undocumented oral form. But publishing history now provides evidence for a beginning, and with it, a scaffolding for a new history of fairy tales. Publishing history, which forms the backbone of the following chapters, does not require a folk invention of fairy tales in a distant and misty past or a folk dissemination of those same tales in early modern Europe.

CONCLUSIONS

Restoration fairy tales grew seamlessly out of the medieval romances that preceeded them, retaining their chivalric locations, courtly activities, and royal characters. Precursor plots about the restoration of displaced and suffering royal figures who returned to their rightful position are nearly as old as storytelling itself, as are many of the motifs that characterize restoration fairy tales. In the 1500s this traditional plot took on a new and abbreviated form as brief tales of princes and princesses whose expulsion and suffering are relieved by magic and marriage.

Rise fairy tales incorporated many ancient motifs, which has made it appear that they were associated with an ancient past where those same motifs had also existed. As they were composed in the 1500s, however, rise tales are brief, secular narratives, with a plotline altogether new to the history of European secular narratives. They incorporate poor protagonists whose lives take on the lineaments of royal heroes and heroines as they sally forth, withstand tests, endure sufferings, and successfully meet trials. In addition, when rise fairy tales first appeared, they were quintessentially for and about people living in cities. Urban creations, their heros and heroines walked on streets, gathered on piazzas, and set out from cities for adventures in distant parts.

Straparola put both restoration and rise fairy tales into his collection, and—translated into French—they were printed in Lyons and Paris for nearly fifty years. New and revised versions of some of those tales, together with two score newly created ones, were published in Naples, their city origins emphasized in an unifying frame tale inhabited and informed by Naples' poorest inhabitants. Fifty years later fairy tales surfaced again, in Paris, as a self-conscious literary genre. A city phenomenon, indeed. The man who was central to the history of fairy tales came, like many of his compatriots, from a small town to a large city to make his fortune. At the end of his life he created a handful of rise fairy tales in which poor girls or boys were helped by magic to a royal marriage that made them wealthy. The new plot that Straparola hit upon in Venice, rags through magic to a marriage and riches, became the most enduringly popular plot for modern fairy tales.[32]

If this were a conventional history of fairy tales, it would begin by stating that fairy tales were originally produced by an anonymous country folk thousands of years ago[33] and were passed along orally,[34] unchanged over generations, unchanged even as a tale such as "Puss in Boots," which first appeared in Venice,[35] made its way over the Alps to France.[36] Such a book would continue by explaining that the many French grandmothers who are known to have told a story like "Puss in Boots" to their grandchildren were part of the same unlettered oral tradition. However, the reasoning in this book is steered by newly examined evidence, and the history it lays out explores the extraordinary success of the fairy tale genre and finds a close association between sales of fairy tale books and a knowledge of fairy tales among the people. When it looks at the many grandmothers who told "Puss in Boots" to their grandchildren in France in the seventeenth and eighteenth centuries, it sees the thousands of French-language books in which it had been published in one French city or another during those grandmothers' lifetimes. It looks at the Grimm brothers and sees two men who believed deeply in the project of creating a single coherent nation from a nearly impossible mix of languages, cultures, and political units and who believed that fairy tales were part of a vast folk creation that underlay the nation they wanted to see strong and united.

Fairy Tales: A New History is a history in reverse. It begins in the nineteenth century, with familiar Grimm fairy tales, and then digs beneath those tales in search of their foundations. A study like this one could have equally well begun in the later nineteenth century, by which time nearly all of Europe had been saturated with national collections of fairy tales. England, for instance, enthusiastically incorporated fairy tales and tales about fairies into its national culture.[37] But it was the early nineteenth-century German tales published by Jacob and Wilhelm Grimm that gave so powerful an impetus to the creation of other national tale collections and to the theories of folk and fairy tales that followed hard on their heels.

The following chapters show that the German fairy tales in the Grimm collection rest on a rich layer of French fairy tales, beneath which there are Italian ones. The process unearths words that were written and stories that were read again and again and again, in a few cases from the sixteenth century straight through to the twenty-first.[38] The short answer to the question, "Why a new history of fairy tales?" is that newly emerging evidence supports a new and vastly different history of fairy tales.

TWO ACCOUNTS OF THE GRIMMS' TALES

The Folk as Creator, The Book as Source

INTRODUCTION

Today the Grimms' tales fill two fairly thick volumes, but in 1812, after five years of collecting, Jacob and Wilhelm Grimm had found only enough tales for one small book. They published that single volume for the Christmas season of 1812, that is, the twelve days of Christmas from 25 December 1812 to 6 January 1813. In the next two years they found more tales and published them for the Christmas season of 1814–1815. For two centuries the tales published by Jacob and Wilhelm Grimm, together with the brothers' explanations about the tales' origins, set the course for understanding the nature of fairy tales for both scholars and ordinary readers.

There are two dissimilar histories of Jacob and Wilhelm Grimm and their tales. Both histories share many of the same characters. Both have several facts in common. But the conclusions that can be and *are* drawn from those facts diverge fundamentally from one another.

For nineteenth- and twentieth-century historians of literature there were many empty spaces in the history of the Grimms'
tales. In part, the empty spaces reflected things that weren't then
known, or then knowable, about the history of fairy tales.
Nonetheless, from the early nineteenth century onward, scholars
filled those empty spaces, and they did so with assertions about
folk origins and an oral spread of fairy tales that were both
undocumented and undocumentable. For more than 150 years
those assertions increased in number and in vigor and became
the basis for and the substance of a history of folk creation and
oral transmission of fairy tales. This is the history that everyone
in the English-speaking world knows. In it there is some truth,
but also much error.

THE OLD HISTORY OF THE GRIMMS' TALES
(AND OF FAIRY TALES IN GENERAL)

Numerous authors have written books about the history of the
Grimms and of their tales. Usually they begin with the first
volume's informants, who were—for the most part—girls and
young women in Jacob's and Wilhelm's social circle in the small
central German town of Cassel. When they began collecting in
1807, Jacob was 22 and Wilhelm 21.

Wilhelm's informants were as young as 14-year-old Dortchen
Wild, one of six daughters of the town apothecary Rudolf Wild
who lived across the street from the Grimm family. Dortchen's
older sister Gretchen, another tale contributor, was 20. The two
girls and their mother told Wilhelm several folk tales and many
fairy tales, some of which—like "The Frog Prince," "Frau Holle,"
"The Six Swans," and "Many Furs"—later became well-known
in the English-speaking world. They also passed on lesser-known
but nonetheless influential tales such as "Mary's Child" and
"The Singing Bones."[1] Wilhelm, always sentimental, made notations about how and where he'd gotten some of the tales. In his

own copy of the 1812 First Edition he wrote in the margin next to "The Singing Bones" that Dortchen had told it to him while they sat together "by the wood-burning stove in the garden house in Nentershausen."[2]

The three Hassenpflug girls, daughters of a socially elevated and politically conservative banking family, were Jacob's principal source. In 1809 when he first met Marie (1788–1856), Jeannette (1791–1860), and Amalie (1800–1871), they ranged in age from 21 to 9. The three girls provided Jacob with dozens of tales, the best-known of which are "The Seven Ravens," "Red Riding Hood," "The Girl Without Hands," "The Robber Bridegroom" (a German equivalent of Charles Perrault's "Blue Beard"), "Sleeping Beauty," "King Thrushbeard," "Snow White," and "The Carnation."[3]

Friederike Mannel (1783–1833), a pastor's daughter in nearby Allendorf who provided five tales in 1808–1809, was another early contributor to their first volume, as were the Ramus sisters Julia (1792–1862) and Charlotte (1793–1858).[4] The Ramus sisters' real significance, however, was that they introduced the Grimms to Dorothea Viehmann (1755–1815), the most important informant for the second volume of the *Nursery and Household Tales* (Kinder- und Hausmärchen).[5]

Because of their sheer number, the tales and tale fragments recounted by Dorothea Viehmann dominated the Grimms' second volume. Unlike Jacob's and Wilhelm's Cassel *Kaffeeklatsch* companions, Frau Viehmann seemed to have genuine non-bourgeois credentials: she was a drover's daughter and a tailor's wife. So central was she to Volume 2 that the Grimms had their younger brother Ludwig Emil draw her likeness for its frontispiece.

Volume 2 also incorporated a stream of stories sent to Jacob and Wilhelm from the farming estate of the Haxthausens. Little Anna (1800–1877), barely into her teens, assiduously submitted bits and pieces, an enterprise in which her older brother August (1792–1866) and sister Ludowine (1795–1872) joined.[6] The

Droste-Hülshoffs contributed tales, too, with young Jenny (1795–1859) particularly enthusiastic.

Traditional accounts of the Grimm tales wax ecstatic about their folk origins. Six months before the tales were printed Wilhelm himself had declared to a Danish literary figure Rasmus Nyerup that their only source had been oral tradition.[7] This assertion of folk origins doesn't square with the apparent facts of the Grimms' actual collecting from the urban Wild girls, the privileged Hassenpflug sisters, and the educated Mannel and Ramus daughters, and so the traditional version of the history of the Grimms' tales has long reconfigured these young women into simple conduits from the folk to the waiting pens of Jacob and Wilhelm Grimm. The brothers themselves are described as faithfully transcribing and transmitting the imperiled tales—imperiled because knowledge of them was believed to be fast dying out—to a grateful posterity.

It is easy to demonstrate the folk origins of Dorothea Viehmann and of other genuine folk contributors to Volume 2 such as Johann Friedrich Krause (c.1750–after 1827), a former sergeant-major in the Hessian Army.[8] But unlike Frau Viehmann's tales, for the most part *his* rough and tumble contributions didn't make it into the collection.

Traditional histories of the Grimms' tales didn't try to establish a direct connection between the Cassel girls and the surrounding countryside. This could not have been an oversight, since it would have been patently clear to anyone who read the girls' and young womens' letters and diaries that none of them frequented pigsties or cowbyres. Neither did they wander into peasant dooryards or set foot in farmers' cottages.

In the absence of a direct connection between the Grimms' girls and countryside folk knowledge, historians of fairy tales turned to an indirect connection, household servants. Nearly every household in Germany's middling classes had servants, and for decades tradition-minded scholars pounded on the possibility that domestics in the Wild, Hassenpflug, and Ramus households stood behind the sisters, daughters, and wives who provided folk and fairy tales to the Grimm brothers. Over time, this possibility turned into a certainty. But in actual fact, with the exception of one servant in the Wild household whose name is known, no information about the age or background of any of the Cassel domestics has come down to us, including whether they were country lasses or city girls.

Nonetheless, the traditional history of fairy tales credits invisible servants and undocumented folk sources with passing tales for the first volume of the Grimm collection from Germany's humble milkmaids, goosegirls, ploughmen, shepherds, drovers, and soldiers through the Grimms' young lady friends in Cassel to the Grimms themselves. In the *second* volume of *Nursery and Household Tales* the problem didn't exist, because there actually were real folk sources who contributed tales to the Grimms. The vast majority of tales from these documentable folk sources were appropriately enough folk tales, not fairy tales.[9] Later scholars projected these folk informants back onto the bourgeois sources of the first volume, a disingenuous practice that allowed the folk to be understood as the source of all the Grimms' tales, even if, in fact, the informants for many of the best known fairy tales were from an urban middle class.

Long decades passed, during which it would have been possible to verify, or to disprove, the belief that folk sources had provided the fairy tales of Volume 1 as well as those of Volume 2. There were, after all, Germany's well-maintained archives, but no one did so. In World War II bombings destroyed the whole of Cassel's municipal records, and afterward it became impossible either to verify or to disprove who lived in individual households and where they had come from. All that remains is Wilhelm Grimm's prefatory description of the collecting process. This text made it easy to create a folk-based history, because in his preface, Wilhelm changed the names of the actual informants (which he had penned into his own copy of the tales) into geographical locations, such as "the Main and Kinzig River region."

One imagined nursemaid in particular was crucial to the argument that oral tradition underlay the Grimms' tales. Identified as "Old Marie" (because Wilhelm had written that name next to several tales in the first volume), she was credited as the folk source for a large number of that volume's fairy tales or parts of tales. Indeed, Herman Grimm (1828–1901), Wilhelm's older son, confirmed her folk identity to everyone's satisfaction at the end of the nineteenth century.

Because a person named "Old Marie" had contributed so many tales to Volume 1, and because one scholar after another identified "Old Marie" as a servant in the Wild household, the person called "Old Marie" became emblematic of the richness of German folk tradition. And because, moreover, many of "Old Marie's" fairy tales faithfully reproduced ones in the European narrative tradition that had been published decades or centuries earlier, she was claimed as Exhibit A for a growing belief that peasants were able to maintain stories in their original form, unchanged even over generations of oral retellings. This was a belief that was shaken only in the 1980s when Heinz Rölleke's revisionist scholarship began to challenge belief in the folk origins of the Grimm tales. (See below, page 46–48.)

The term Märchen is the German word for brief narrative, and the Grimms had their own history and understanding of it. To make sense of their conception of Märchen, however, it's necessary to understand that their collection consists of a broad range of short narratives. A great many were folk tales of one sort or another (animal tales, tales of origins, religious legends, jests, burlesques, and moral tales). A few were tales about fairy-land, and several were fairy tales. (See chapter 1 for definitions of these differing kinds of tales.)

Wilhelm's rambling prefaces laid the foundation for the traditional history of fairy tales as orally produced and spread, and in so doing he set the direction for most research down to the present day. According to him, Märchen were a natural phenomenon, that is, part of Nature itself. Märchen were the plants whose seeds had fallen into hedgerows or hidden places and had managed to survive an all-destructive storm of political events and social change—Wilhelm's coded reference to Napoleon's devastating invasion and (in 1812 and 1813) ongoing occupation of the Germanies.[10]

As for his informants, Wilhelm transformed the Cassel girls and young women who had told him tales by often removing their personal names, erasing their urban lives, turning them into German geographical entities, and referring to them collectively as "oral tradition in Hesse and in the Main and Kinzig River valleys in the county of Hanau."[11] These geographical areas were also the settings of the Grimms' own childhood: Hanau where they had been born, the Kinzig River Valley where they had spent a few happy childhood years, and the Electorate of Hesse-Cassel with Cassel as its capital, where they had grown to young manhood. In the preface to the *Nursery and Household Tales*, Wilhelm explicitly identified himself and Jacob with this geographical provenance.[12]

As far as the tales' survival was concerned, Wilhelm suggested conscious intention and purpose on the part of higher powers when he called tradition bearers "those who are meant to preserve [the tales]."[13] Wilhelm visualized those intended preservers for his readers by extending the image of hedgerows that safeguarded stray grain seeds against the storm of an encroaching modernity. Metaphorizing and personifying that image, Wilhelm moved it beyond the hedgerows to the surrounding land and rural occupations and brought it indoors into the realm of household, servant-performed activities, even into the tranquil minds of the humblest humans: "The hedges that have safeguarded [the tales] and have transmitted them from one era to another have been the stools around the woodstove, the kitchen hearth, the attic stairs, holidays that people still celebrate, pastures, the woods in their stillness, and above all, undisturbed imaginations."[14] None of these metaphors applied in the smallest way to the real girls and women who had sat around coffee tables in

parlors or garden houses when they told the stories that Jacob
and Wilhelm wrote down. They applied only to the folk that
Wilhelm envisaged: those who served ("woodstove" and
"hearth") and those who lived in household "attics," those who
herded geese, cows, and pigs in pastures, and those who burned
charcoal in the "woods."

Wilhelm provided an instant ancestry for the tales he and
Jacob had collected when he defined them as part of "everything
that still exists from Germany's ancient poetic forms."[15] It's easy
to understand the presence of a desire, conscious or not, to assert
the continuing existence of a coherent and unifying German
past, when in his corner of Germany a French occupation force
confronted him at every step he took outside his home. But
between a desire for national identity and cultural cohesion, and
the history he proposed that would provide that identity and
that cohesion, there was a yawning divide.

Wilhelm also laid the groundwork for associating the tales of
his and Jacob's collection with children, childhood, and the
childhood of humanity by creating images of childness to characterize the tales themselves. "The same purity that makes children seem so miraculous and soulful to us perfuses these poetic
creations. The tales have the same milky-white, unblemished,
shining eyes."[16] By associating the *Nursery and Household Tales*
with the childhood of humanity, Wilhelm extended the history
of the tales they had collected beyond the middle ages into an
undated and undatable ancient past.

At the same time Wilhelm created an urgent immediacy for
his tales by relating contemporary human experience to details
from their plots. In so doing he set the stage for the still prevailing popular conviction that the *Nursery and Household Tales* had
proceeded directly from peasants' lives. In conversationally frag-
mentary style, Wilhelm alluded to narrative events and episodes
and implied that they corresponded to daily folk experience:
"Parents are out of bread and have to drive their children out, or
else an unfeeling stepmother makes them suffer,[17] and would like

to have them destroyed." Wilhelm introduced and sometimes interpreted choice bits from the tales in fragmented musings: "There are siblings abandoned in the lonely woods, the wind terrifies them, fear of wild beasts, but they support each other in complete loyalty, the little brother knows how to find the way home again, or the little sister, when magic transforms her brother, leads him—now changed into a little fawn—and searches out herbs for him and moss for a place to sleep; or she sits silently, and sews a shirt of starworts that will destroy the enchantment."[18]

The tales had not been authored, Wilhelm believed. Instead, he felt that they were anonymous narratives that had arisen from shared experience and perceptions, because "spoken documents that are in themselves so rich with their own analogies or reminiscences . . . couldn't have been invented."[19] By "invented," Wilhelm seems to have meant "created by urban genius." Wilhelm conflated narrative and narrator, teller and author, content and subject, and in so doing he and Jacob conceptualized a theory from which to create a history of folk and fairy tales.

Wilhelm set in place an enduring Romantic notion about a storytelling folk whose stories remained constant from one generation to another. He posited a background thrum in folk culture, a storytelling that united the disparate Germanies' diverse peoples into a single coherent culture. In this imagined past, tales became animate for him. They had, he wrote, "constantly regenerated themselves in the course of time. . ."[20] Wilhelm's statement is so simple that it might easily be read past and overlooked, but it should be lingered over, because it has been profoundly influential in fairy tale scholarship. His statement meant, for instance, that oral tradition, that is, oral tellings of fairy tales and folk tales, moral tales and religious tales, tales of origins, jests, and anecdotes were, and had always been, an integral part of folk culture. He came to this conclusion because many tales they were being told resembled tales that had been published in the distant past.

The only way that Wilhelm could account for the similarity between a tale told at the Hassenpflugs in the nineteenth century and a tale published by sixteenth-century writers like Johannes Fischart (1546–1590) and Georg Rollenhagen (1542–1609) was to conclude that both they themselves as well as Fischart and Rollenhagen had dipped into one and the same everlasting oral tradition. Initially the Grimms knew nothing of the scores of books that had kept those stories alive between the sixteenth and the nineteenth centuries. Later, when they did learn something of that sort, they had already formed their views. To the present day a tradition-based history of fairy tales has maintained Wilhelm's views and has assumed that the kinds of tales that appear in the Grimm collection had always existed and that they had survived, because they had constantly and continuously regenerated themselves, mysteriously and unaccountably remaining unchanged and elemental, because of their ability to recreate themselves in their own image. Wilhelm stated this in his preface[21]; it has remained a central tenet of folklore-based and much literary fairy tale research ever since; and generations of folk narrative scholars have created "Laws" that affirm the same view.[22]

Wilhelm was never able to date fairy tales to any point earlier than Straparola's sixteenth-century ones, but despite that, he claimed a chronologically open-ended past for their history. For Wilhelm it followed logically that something like the fund of tales that he understood as orally transmitted and self-regenerating would not have sprung into the world of sixteenth- or seventeenth-century narrative *de novo*. For him, the tales were "doubtless . . . far older, even though," he conceded, "an absence of references to them makes direct proofs impossible."[23] Wilhelm's central error was to apply the same term both to folk tales with an ancient history that could be documented as well as to the kinds of fairy tales that had a documented history of less than 300 years (at the time at which Wilhelm was writing). In so doing he wittingly or unwittingly grafted the history of ancient folk tales onto the history of early modern fairy tales, and first implied and later claimed that the relatively new fairy tales were as old as the genuinely ancient folk tales.

Just as Wilhelm ignored or glossed over historical limits in his description of folk and fairy tales, he also erased geographical boundaries. In the case of geography, however, he had evidence that he considered sound, because he had located tales of the sort he was collecting in Denmark, Norway and Sweden, England and Wales, Spain, France, and Italy.[24] These tales, which closely resembled one another, came from published books, and with nothing else to go on, Wilhelm assumed that a great sea of story had tossed its *Märchen* onto many shores, even ones that were far distant from one another.

This description of Wilhelm's musings on the history of fairy tales reflects the preface he wrote for Volume 1 of the 1812 First Edition, whose direct contributors, I'll mention once again, were principally bourgeois acquaintances and fellow intellectuals. When, in Volume 2, he referred to his genuine folk source, the fifty-year-old Dorothea Viehmann from the nearby village of Zwehrn, his enthusiasm was boundless and his convictions were even stronger. Frau Viehmann's sturdy constitution, her strong but pleasant features, her clear gaze, and her probable youthful beauty made her a perfect representative of German-ness in Wilhelm's eyes.[25] More remarkable was her uncanny memory. She could repeat a story time after time in exactly the same words. She could speed up or slow down. Her performance, he said, would persuade any skeptic that oral transmission could channel a narrative unchanged from one era to another, because she, Frau Viehmann, never changed a word in her tellings, and if she made a mistake, she corrected it the next time around.[26] From Wilhelm's observations of Frau Viehmann's storytelling ability and style, it was but a short step to a far-reaching generalization about a central difference between the folk and educated people like him, his brother, and their Cassel friends. People like Frau Viehmann were solid and unchanging, their lives determined by ancient usage and living tradition: "The devotion to traditional material among people who lived as they have always done is stronger than we comprehend, we who tend towards change."[27]

Frau Viehmann's abilities gave rise to an unshakeable belief in *Volksdichtung*,[28] people's literature or oral literature. It was a concept that enabled Wilhelm first to link medieval epics to modern fairy tales and then to equate them with one another. For Wilhelm the sleeping princess of "Briar Rose" had once been the slumbering Brunhilde. Similarly, the white-skinned and black-haired Snow White was simply the medieval Snäfridr, and Snow White's coffin the same one by which a medieval Haraldur had sat for three long years.[29] In this way, the fairy tales that Jacob and Wilhelm were collecting became evidence for the existence of *Volks=Märchen* long believed to have been lost, in a period long before they had been documented. Wilhelm and his brother were now convinced that a broad search would turn up more survivals from early times.[30]

Wilhelm wrote, and believed, that the tales not only embodied German-ness, but that they showed Germans how to be German. Their tale collection was, in his words, a training manual, an *Erziehungsbuch* as he called it, that was as natural as nature itself.[31] Or, he proposed, one might think of these tales as "rain and dew" benefiting everything upon which they fell.[32]

At the end of the preface to Volume 2, Wilhelm explained his and Jacob's critical method. Narrative variants would be included in their appended notes.[33] Nothing had been or would be changed, nor would anything be altered. Moreover, everything was genuinely German, with the single exception of "Puss in Boots,"[34] which, in any case, was removed from the next edition because of its French origins.

Four years later, even though 350 copies (of the original 900-volume print run) of the folk-based Volume 2 of the First Edition still lay unsold on warehouse shelves in Berlin, Wilhelm persuaded his publisher Georg Reimer to produce a Second Edition.[35] In this edition Wilhelm joined the two separate prefaces of volumes 1 and 2 into one. This had the effect of applying his remarks about folk tales (so amply represented in Volume 2) equally to fairy tales (so many of which appeared in Volume 1). He thoroughly edited the resulting preface for content and style, shifting from his former conversational mode to a more formal tone and removing what he considered extraneous material. The most significant excision was his erasure of assertions that since country folk hadn't read Italian, French, or Oriental books, they could not have been privy to tales in those languages, and that the tales in the collection were therefore purely German and not borrowed from other cultures.[36] In making this statement Wilhelm chose to overlook significant and relevant phenomena: 1) the extent to which country individuals could read; 2) the practice of reading aloud that was particularly strong in the country and that has been so well documented in recent years; 3) the translations of French and Italian fairy tales into German in the eighteenth century; and 4) the initially ironic presentation of French fairy tales as German ones told by the German folk.[37] Thereafter—in the prefaces to the Third, Fourth, and Fifth Large Editions—Wilhelm made few revisions to the concepts he had finalized in the 1819 preface to the Second Edition. The Preface to the Sixth Large Edition incorporated an expanded bibliography of book sources for *Märchen* from dozens of foreign and exotic lands, musings on changes in the public's response to their collection, large numbers of tale summaries, and thoughts on the relationship between German and Indogermanic tales, nearly all of which became part of the scholarly apparatus in volume 3 (1856) of the Final Large Edition, whose publication preceded Volumes 1 and 2 (1857) by one year. This material has disappeared from the Prefaces section of the scholarly edition of the Grimms' tales most commonly used in the 1980s and 1990s, the 3–volume reprint of the 1857 edition prepared by Heinz Rölleke. He probably wished, and reasonably so, to avoid a lengthy repetition, because it appears in Volume 3. Still, its absence from the Prefaces section means that contemporary readers remain

unaware that Wilhelm put a huge amount of his personal
thought about *Märchen* front and center at the beginning of the
Sixth Large Edition. In addition to the Prefaces of the seven
Large and ten Small Editions of the Grimms' tales that were published between 1812 and 1858, Wilhelm also penned prefaces for
the volumes of scholarly apparatus that appeared in 1822 and
1856, the first of which implies emphatically an omnipresence of
Märchen of all sorts, which tacitly included fairy tales.

Wilhelm died in 1859, Jacob a few years later in 1863. In the
following generation countless appreciations of their work
appeared. Appraisals of a scholarly sort began only toward the
end of the nineteenth century, some thirty years after their
deaths. The late nineteenth century was an era of all-embracing
and universal theories, and so it is not surprising that one scholarly approach drew on the cosmos and related tales to planetary
movements as they would have been perceived by the simple
folk. In this theory "Red Riding Hood" was a fictionalization of
primitive people's observations that the red dawn (Red Riding
Hood) emerges on a daily basis from nocturnal obscurity (the
wolf's belly). For a nation that had just defeated the French in
the Franco-Prussian war of 1870, such an interpretation also
enabled them to dismiss Perrault's "Red Riding Hood" as frivolous, even though his French story was a morality tale in which
the heroine remained irretrievably in the belly of the devouring
wolf, a powerful reminder for young girls to avoid two-legged as
well as four-legged wolves.

Nineteenth-century educators' use of the Grimms' tales were
more plausible. In search of school readings for the children of
Germany's growing urban proletariat, Germany's educational
establishments turned to the Grimms' tales as examples of the
Germanic spirit that Wilhelm had identified and had wished to
foster. Beginning in the 1830s, the Grimms' tales were built into
German elementary school curricula, with the result that by the
end of the nineteenth century, first-year pupils were memorizing
the simplest tales and older pupils were explicating the longer and

more complex ones.[38] After World War II Germany's Allied conquerors evidently shared Wilhelm Grimm's view that tales in the collection could and would impart Germanness to the German nation, and in 1945 Allied Forces banned the Grimm tales as a whole from school curricula in Germany, removed copies of the tales from school and library shelves, and shipped them abroad, many to American municipal and university libraries.

When literary study of the Grimms' tales emerged in early twentieth-century Germany, a hundred years had passed since the tales' first publication in 1812/13 and 1815. In the early twentieth century, literary scholars accepted Wilhelm's prefaces at face value, and Wilhelm's assumptions became scholars' assertions. Wilhelm had said he'd changed nothing essential. That was understood as the Grimms having changed nothing substantial. Eventually that notion turned into a belief that the Grimms had changed nothing at all.[39] The last statement made the brothers into the world's first scholarly and scientific folklorists, transcribers of folk language, intimates of folk culture,[40] witnesses to and preservers of the final stage of a millenia-long process of oral transmissions. Nothing could have been further from the truth about the bookish brothers. Neither made it a practice to go among the folk in search of tales. Their preferred venue was one in which they were seated comfortably at a Biedermeier table, coffee near to hand.

The Grimms' diligence and genius had already become a frequently mentioned and always celebrated reference point in the nineteenth century, a shorthand for highly esteemed and (by imputation) peculiarly German virtues. In the course of such celebrations of the Grimms themselves, the Märchen itself, the "tale," was defined in vivid and instantly comprehensible imagery, and the term Märchen (which embraced so many kinds of tales) was inaccurately and misleadingly translated into English as "fairy tale." Grimm scholars reformulated the positivist thinker Auguste Comte's unbroken chain linking the ancient past to the contemporary world into an image congruent with

Wilhelm and Jacob Grimm's understanding of the history of the tales in their collection. The result was the development of an unyielding orthodoxy, in which an infinite number of invariant tellings, each a link in a chain from the ancient world to the present time, had carried tales from the childhood of humanity, that is, from some period that preceded ancient Greece, down to the present day, or at least to the Grimms' own day.

A second image associated with "tales" in general hardened into an equally firm belief. Arising from an Indic theory of origins, this was the one already-mentioned image which had been given to a collection of tales from the Indian subcontinent, *The Ocean of Story*. In this theoretical model, tales in the vast sea of stories washed over all shores in the world, so that Germans, Frenchmen, or Italians dipping their nets into that sea would haul out the same catch of stories. They were everywhere the same, because—as the traditional history of fairy tales explained—starting from an unknown origin, the world's folk had transmitted these stories orally to every corner of the world. No one had ever recorded the folk telling *fairy* tales before the nineteenth century, but the imputed and assumed orality of the storytelling process made documentation an irrelevance. What was obviously and documentably true for folk tales was assumed to be true for fairy tales as well. As a consequence, literary fairy tales came to be seen as contaminations of what was considered to have been a pure oral tradition. Over time, folk narrative theory not only accepted an absence of evidence for their theories as far as fairy tales were concerned; it relied, and even insisted on, an absence of evidence, and in so doing it created "fairy tales about fairy tales."[41]

THE GRIMMS AND THEIR WORLD

A dispassionate look at the lives of the two Grimm brothers and a close consideration of the world within which they collected tales puts their literary work into a meaningful historical context. Jacob and Wilhelm were the oldest of six surviving siblings—five boys and one girl. They were born to the wife of a magistrate for the German Calvinist ruler of Hesse-Cassel. In the Grimms' day, German Calvinists were still called *Reformiert*, an adjectival noun that not only distinguished them from Lutherans but also carried strong connotations of educational and social superiority. The Grimms' was a sober and solid household, heir to generations of Calvinist, that is, German Reformed, clergymen. Their official residence in Steinau was similarly solid, sober, and imposing. But when their father died in 1796 their childhood comfort and security disappeared overnight. At the tender age of eleven Jacob had to take on family responsibilities from a mother who was frequently indisposed.

Steinau offered no suitable education for the now-poor Jacob and Wilhelm. Off to Cassel they went, sent by their mother to the oversight of her sister, a lady-in-waiting to the Hessian Margrave's wife. Lodged with the court cook, the boys had a life of hard study, few pleasures, and fewer advantages. Although prepared by gymnasium studies for their higher education, they barely gained admission to the University of Marburg, which was then a preserve for scions of noble houses. The Grimms' borderline social class also denied them financial support, since the university reserved its financial gifts for sons of the nobility.

Nonetheless, first Jacob, and then Wilhelm, began the study of law at Marburg. Their hard times there were softened by their acquaintance with a young professor of Roman law, Friedrich von Savigny. From a wealthy landowning family, he possessed a generations-old family library of books and manuscripts, which he generously made available to the young and enthusiastic Grimms. It was in Savigny's library that the two brothers found their lifework.[42] Instead of professionally practicing law after their university studies, as their family had fondly hoped, both brothers became librarians for the Margrave of Cassel. Their pay was a pittance, but on it they fed and housed their mother, brothers, and sister Lotte, though often barely above a subsistence level.

When Napoleon invaded the Germanies, the Grimms' world changed abruptly. The Margrave fled with his court, and Napoleon installed his brother Jérôme as King of Westphalia. The new king appointed Jacob—because of his excellent command of French—to serve as secretary of a war-related commission. In 1808 Jacob applied for and was awarded the royal librarianship, which he held until late in 1813, when the French were driven out.

Jacob's generous stipend from the hated conqueror's hands points towards a set of rarely discussed consequences. It was around Napoleon's invasion of the Germanies that a German national consciousness coalesced. In Cassel Jérôme's occupation sharply focused the Grimms' awareness of Germanic literature. Moreover, the generous salary the detested invader paid Jacob between 1808 and 1813 supported the Grimms' participation in Cassel's middle and upper class society. A literary paradox ensued. The tales that the Grimms garnered for Volume 1, the beginning of their literary effort to create German-ness, show by far a greater connection with tales that had entered Germany from France than they do with any tales of German origin.[43]

As the Grimm brothers began working on Volume 2 of their tale collection in 1813, conditions in Hesse-Cassel changed again within the politico-historical context of early nineteenth-century Europe. In late 1813 Napoleon lost a crucial battle near Leipzig; King Jérôme Bonaparte abruptly left Cassel; and the German Margrave returned. Jacob, whose French had made him as useful to the Margrave as he had earlier been to Jérôme Bonaparte, was sent first on a diplomatic mission to Paris and then on another to the Congress of Vienna.

In Jacob's absence Wilhelm became secretary in the Margrave's library.[44] It was in this period that the market vendor Dorothea Viehmann became a major contributor to their collection, an experience that solidified Wilhelm Grimm's views of tales of all sorts (*Märchen*), including fairy tales. His experience with Frau Viehmann also created the foundation for two hundred years of fairy tale studies based on the mistaken belief that an anonymous and illiterate folk had created fairy tales and passed them on from generation to generation.

A NEW HISTORY OF GRIMMS' TALES

The Grimms themselves were poor judges of the folk that they claimed to be the pure creators of and the uncontaminated disseminators of oral narrative. In the years of their collecting for the first volume of the First Edition, Wilhelm and Jacob must have been remarkably ignorant about Germany's folk. Despite the personal poverty of their adolescent years in Cassel and their early adult years in Marburg and again in Cassel, they had passed their childhood among Hesse-Cassel's privileged and had spent their early manhood in libraries and archives, and, when ill health forced it, in spas. Unworldly, inexperienced, and like the tales they recorded, generally innocent of sexual knowledge, they were personally naïve about the peasantry's earthy world. Thus it is not surprising that they projected the simplicity with which they were personally familiar onto the tales they were collecting, and beyond them, to the folk they believed in. Nothing demonstrates their own ignorance of folk humor so well as their inclusion of a folktale called "Mrs. Fox's Wedding" in the *Nursery and Household Tales*:

> A fox with nine tails feigned death to see how his wife would react. As soon as word got out that Herr Fox had died, suitors arrived to woo Frau Fox. When the first arrived, Frau Fox asked her maid if he had nine beautiful tails as had her dear departed husband. Only one tail, came the answer, so she rejected him immediately. The next had two, then came one with three, and so on.

Each was turned away until the ninth arrived, and he, oh glory, had nine tails, so she told her maid to get rid of her husband's corpse and prepare to celebrate. With the guests' arrival, however, her husband suddenly revived and drove everyone from the house, including his faithless wife.[45]

It seems a harmless enough story except that *Schwanz*, the word for the "tail" that Frau Fox wanted nine of, was—and is—German slang for "penis." That casts the story in an entirely different light, and indeed, the Grimms' friend Achim von Arnim admonished them about this lewd tale, blaming its leering sexuality on "French wantonness."[46] Jacob hotly denied von Arnim's assertions that "Mrs. Fox's Wedding" was a dirty story, because he'd heard it as something innocently funny when he was little and had never understood it in any other way. The innocence with which the Grimms—and Jacob in particular—credited the folk was in fact their own. Eventually, when Wilhelm turned to early German published sources to augment his collection, he faced head-on a German print tradition of brutal violence, repellent scatology, and raw sex that must have modified his view of folk purity, though—in fact—he never changed the wording of his prefaces to reflect any change in his expressed views of folk innocence and purity.

In the early 1980s there was still near universal agreement among Grimm scholars that Jacob and Wilhelm had gotten their tales from the folk and that they had handed all of these tales on, unchanged, to subsequent generations. Occasionally voices were raised against this orthodoxy, but in terms of affecting the way people understood that the Grimms had actually edited the tales in their collection, it was John Ellis who raised an alarum in the English-speaking world.

Across the Atlantic in Germany, Heinz Rölleke was paying close attention to the details of the Grimm brothers' social life. His work resulted in documented names and dates that undermined belief in the tales' unalloyed folk history. Next, Rölleke began to edit the Grimms' *Nursery and Household Tales* and to reprint various editions, first the final Large Edition of 1857, together with Wilhelm's notations and essays on *Märchen*, along with his (Rölleke's) own observations on the tales' origins, the year and edition of the first appearance of each tale that appeared in the Final Large Edition, a comprehensive listing of contributors' names and the titles (or contents) of their contributions, and a lengthy afterword. Then Rölleke turned to the beginning of the tales' editing history and republished the First Edition of 1812 and the Ölenberg Manuscript of 1810. His close study of the 1810 and 1812 collections led him to doubt the traditional history of peasant origins and oral transmission, and a new narrative began to emerge.

Using Wilhelm's own copy of the First Edition in Cassel's Grimm Archive, Rölleke noted its spidery marginalia, in particular Wilhelm's attributions of tales to named individuals—Dortchen, Gretchen, Jeannette, Lisette, Male, Marie, and Mie. Wilhelm's son Herman had glossed the names for posterity and in 1895 had vividly identified "Marie" as "Old Marie"[47]: "Dortchen also got her trove from another source. Above the Wilds' nursery in the apothecary building, with its many hallways, stairwells, floors, and rear additions, through all of which I myself poked as a child, was the realm of "Old Marie" . . . One feels immediately that Dortchen and Gretchen probably only recounted what had been impressed upon them by Old Marie."[48]

At the end of the nineteenth-century and for decades thereafter it bothered no one that Herman Grimm's lively description sprang onto the stage nearly eighty-five years after the old family servant "Old Marie" had left the Wild household. Neither, to our knowledge, did it seem suspicious to anyone that Herman's tardy description was the first and only one of that reputedly storytelling servant. After another eighty-five years or so had passed, however, Heinz Rölleke wondered how Herman had known anything at all about Old Marie and why he was so sure of his facts.

After all, he reasoned, the "Old Marie" he described had moved away from Cassel in 1812 and had died two years before Herman was born.[49]

Discrepancies and discontinuities in "Old Marie"'s identity spurred on Rölleke's detective work. Using the Grimms' social calendar he calculated the dates on which each of the tales attributed to "Old Marie" had been gathered. He found, surprisingly, that each tale had been written down on a day on which the Grimms had been visiting the Hassenpflug house. This alone undermined the notion that a servant in the *Wild* household named "Old Marie" could be considered a credible source. Eventually Rölleke concluded that "Old Marie" had nothing to do with running the Wild household, but was instead an older Hassenpflug sister named Marie.

The Marie in the Hassenpflug household was born in 1788, and thus 24 or 25 when Volume 1 was published in 1812/1813 and Wilhelm penned her name into the margins of his copy of the *Nursery and Household Tales*. This Marie had attended social gatherings with her sisters and other Grimm acquaintances, her presence on those occasions chronicled by her older brother Ludwig Hassenpflug (1794–1862) in his autobiography.[50]

The evidence Rölleke uncovered had long been available, but such was Herman Grimm's stature both as a leading Germanist and as Wilhelm Grimm's son, and such was the public's desire for the kind of misinformation he had provided that no one seems to have wanted to dig out facts that might contradict his version of the tales' origins among the folk, that is, taken down from a servant storyteller. And indeed, identifying "Old Marie" as yet another educated young woman of the Cassel bourgeoisie dramatically diminished the folk associations and identity of Volume 1. Herman's false identification of "Old Marie" had retarded investigations into the sources of the Grimms' tales by seventy-five years, but when Rölleke recognized a young woman of Cassel's *haute bourgeoisie* as the fictive and folkloric "Old Marie," at a stroke he set the record straight about the immediate source for a large number of contributions that Jacob had recorded.

The battle for the folk was not over, however. If it could be claimed that Marie Hassenpflug had gotten her tales from a nurse-maid in the Hassenpflug household, then 1) scholars could continue to regard her as a neutral conduit from the folk; 2) the tales of "Old Marie" could still be regarded as folk in origin as could the tales by Cassel's other girls and women; and 3) the traditional account of the history of the *Nursery and Household Tales* could remain as it had been. Thus, in and of itself, Rölleke's discovery of Old Marie's real identity changed little. Additional information to support a revision of the old history was needed before the traditional oralist history of fairy tales could be changed.

In the last third of the twentieth century, social historians and historians of book and publishing history began investigating overarching subjects, one of which was German literacy in historical perspective. Literacy was coming to be seen as characterizing the populations of all German cities, Protestant as well as Catholic. And in the countryside, literacy was found to have been widespread throughout Protestant Germany, a significant fact, because it was Protestant informants who supplied Wilhelm with his early tales and in particular with his fairy tales. In addition, the generation before Jacob and Wilhelm's had experienced a popular Enlightenment, a *Volksaufklärung*, which had raised levels of literacy among Catholics as well as among Protestants. All of these newly emerging perceptions began to modify the image of the German folk as a single homogeneous cultural entity of nonliterate, aliterate, or preliterate orally-rooted tellers of fairy tales.

In addition the growing study of book history unqualifiedly supported Rölleke's research into book sources for the Grimms' informants. By the late 1980s and early 1990s, thanks to re-cataloguings carried out electronically, scholars could verify intertextual carryovers from books to oral informants in an increasing number of cases, and the results steadily revealed that the fairy tales of Volume 1—far from originating among an illiterate folk—demonstrated close connections between stories told to Jacob and Wilhelm by their young Cassel friends on the one hand and published European fairy tales on the other. (See chapter 1 for a reminder about distinctions between fairy tales and folk tales.) Indeed, many motifs and plots from traditional and preexisting European fairy tales can be found in the Grimms' first volume of *Nursery and Household Tales*, for example in "The Frog Prince," "Mary's Child," "The Twelve Brothers," "Rapunzel," "The White Serpent," "Cinderella," "Frau Holle," "The Seven Ravens," "The Singing Bones," "The Six Swans," "Sleeping Beauty," "King Thrushbeard," "Snow White," "Rumpelstiltskin," "Many Furs," "Jorinde and Joringel," "The Three Lucky Children," "The Carnation," and "The Golden Children." Increasingly, Rölleke and others began to focus attention on earlier incarnations of these stories, and increasingly they concluded that when it came to fairy tales, these stories had come from books read by Cassel's girls and young women in the late eighteenth and early nineteenth centuries.[51]

What the Grimms did not know at the point at which they were attributing folk sources to the stories the bourgeois Wild and Hassenpflug girls were telling them was that these stories had long existed in Germany in print. First in French and later in German, the tales had been available in books for fifty years before the Grimms began collecting.[52] They didn't know this, because they had been brought up in a strict German Reformed household that banned frivolous literature, and their passing acquaintance with current books of fairy tales served principally to fuel their scorn for printed versions.[53] But tales of fantasy and magic had, in fact, occupied a large place among Germany's books for leisure reading from the 1760s onward. Today's scholars have access to many of them in reprints, but in 1812 Wilhelm was aware of only a handful, and the few he knew were clearly insufficient to account for the widespread knowledge of fairy tales he observed among his contemporaries. Hence we should be wary of indicting Wilhelm and Jacob Grimm of intentionally misleading their readers.

Marie Hassenpflug's family had obviously shown a more liberal interest in frivolous books, given the large number of tales of French origin among those the sisters told Wilhelm.[55] The French scholar of German literature Gonthier-Louis Fink early explored French-German interrelationships in terms of fairy tales (1966), and confirmations of German fairy tales' French origins have been documented in a 1988 study by a German archivist, Manfred Grätz, who chronicled in overwhelmingly persuasive detail a long and varied procession of French fairy tales into Germany that began in the mid-1700s and that continued for decades. His study of fairy tales in the German Enlightenment lists hundreds of German imprints, reprints, translations, editings, and re-editings of French tales in Germany and shows their textual relationships to one another.

Grätz's study leads unavoidably to the conclusion that beneath and behind the celebrated Germanic taletelling tradition were the French and their tales about fairies and their fairy tales. The French had been defeated on the battlefields of Leipzig and Jena, but in the fairy tale realm, they prevailed. It was the Napoleonic intrusion that had impelled the Grimms to seek an authentic German identity. What a dénouement to discover in the 1980s that Germany's fairy tales (remember the distinction between fairy and folk tales) were to a very large extent actually French, not *völkisch*, in origin. This conclusion has proved uncomfortable, unpalatable even, and undesireable for many researchers who wish to retain a now outdated oralist history of fairy tales.

Might Wilhelm Grimm have sensed, consciously or unconsciously, the alien origins of the fairy tales he so passionately believed to have been purely German? There are reasons to believe that he did. In a sentence near the end of the preface of the First Edition's second volume, the articulate Wilhelm wrote the highly problematic phrase mentioned earlier: "People customarily trot out reasons [to explain] the borrowing from Italian, French, or Oriental books, which however aren't read by the folk, especially in the country."

Wilhelm speaks here of "borrowing" from "books." This was certainly the case as far as the young ladies in Cassel were concerned. But in his preface he had elided those storytellers in favor of "the folk" by asserting that country folk didn't read books in foreign languages. We are, of course, left wondering if he knew that many of them could read books in German. In an early nineteenth-century Cassel only recently freed from a heavy and hated French yoke, Wilhelm did not want to discuss French (or Italian) tales as sources for German fairy tales. It cannot be accidental that in later prefaces he avoided the subject entirely by simply excising his problematic reference to "borrowing from Italian, French, or Oriental books."

Did country folk, or some among them, actually read German translations of those "Italian, French, or Oriental" books? That is an entirely different question. Grätz's research demonstrates a plentiful existence of French fairy tales rewritten and published for literate German readers in city and country. His bibliographical listings make it theoretically possible to reconstruct, or at least to imagine, the readings of individual informants from the Grimms' social circle in Cassel, although an overarching study of parallels between the contents of scores of books that Grätz cited and the repertoires of individual informants whom the Grimms consulted has yet to be published.

The next chapter will continue its book-based history by demonstrating that the genuinely French Charles Perrault, long credited with taking his tales from his children's nursemaid, lifted most of them directly from books by Giovanfrancesco Straparola and Giambattista Basile.

THREE

THE LATE SEVENTEENTH- AND EIGHTEENTH-CENTURY LAYERS

Perrault, Lhéritier, and Their Successors

BETWEEN THE GRIMMS AND PERRAULT'S WORLD

Chapter 2 discussed two fundamentally differing accounts of the Grimms' tales. The first propounded a non- or illiterate people, an unschooled folk that remembered narrative motifs and episodes from ancient Greece and Rome and incorporated them, along with elements of hoary Germanic mythology, into elaborate fairy tales and tales about fairies. The folk was supposed to have conceived these tales anonymously and to have passed them on in a millennia-long oral tradition to the modern world. The second account places the Grimms' tales in a historical context in which print looms large and literate informants even larger.

For the long eighteenth century that preceded the Grimms' first publication of their tales, there are also two differing accounts. The first is familiar. One hundred and ten years before the Grimms began collecting tales, the Frenchman Charles Perrault consulted the folk and came away from peasant informants, or perhaps from a nursemaid in his household, with a little volume of eight of the best-known and most-loved tales in western Europe: "Sleeping Beauty," "Red Riding Hood," "Blue Beard," "Puss in Boots," "Diamonds and Toads," "Cinderella," "Ricky of the Tuft," and "Little Thumbling." French scholarship typically labels these tales *folklorique*, clearly suggesting that each tale had a folk origin and was intimately associated with the French *peuple*, the native folk. Such scholarly designations reflect assumptions from an entire century of writing about fairy tales and those designations hold—as do most contemporary English, American, and French fairy tale researchers—that Perrault got his tales not from published books but from simple people.

Most scholars similarly claim that family nursemaids, all illiterate peasants, of course, underlay the extraordinary efflorescence of fairy tales in the 1690s and the first years of the 1700s. In these years, they assume, France's sophisticated urban storytellers, the *conteuses* and the *conteurs*, the women and men who met one another in salons and who composed fairy tales, had consulted their unschooled servants and had come away with stories that they turned into their many volumes of subsequently famous tales.[1]

The tales the *conteuses* and *conteurs* published are literarily polished, which traditional accounts explain away in the following manner. The original peasants' tellings had been pure oral narratives passed along from person to person for centuries, but the *conteuses* and *conteurs* had contaminated the peasants' simple tales with literary style and borrowed embellishments, elaborating and embroidering the peasants' genuine tellings. Current scholarship about the relationship between classic fairy tales and a posited peasant oral tradition often offers finely nuanced discussions of what the *conteuses* and *conteurs* added to the putatively popular source, but in the end, that popular source is assumed to have been a nurse or a peasant, and discussions of the origins of France's fairy tales generally join smoothly to the traditional account of the Grimms' *Nursery and Household Tales*, which goes like this: first the Grimms, and before the Grimms,

Perrault and other recorders of peasant fairy tales. This account, however, is contradicted by a growing body of evidence based on book history.

Digging below the Grimm layer turns up a great many literary artifacts, lying for the most part separate from one another. In Germany, some are in fluent German, some are in a stilted and awkward translation into German, and some are in French.[2] Most are for adults, some for children.

For Europe as a whole in the fifty-year layer before the Grimms, one book written by Jeanne-Marie Leprince de Beaumont (1711–1780) recurs frequently, and it does so in several languages. In German it bears the title *Der Frau Maria le Prince de Beaumont Lehren der Tugend und Weisheit für die Jugend*,[3] which translates as *Frau Marie Leprince de Beaumont's Teachings about Virtue and Wisdom for Young People*. Mme Leprince de Beaumont's book, with its moralized fairy tales, was originally published in London in French in 1756 and was subsequently translated from French into German and published both in Switzerland and the Germanies. For the eighteenth century it was a runaway success, republished in German in the 1760s, 70s, and 80s.[4] Nor were Switzerland and Germany the only place that Mme Leprince de Beaumont's book spread the plots of French fairy tales: it was also published frequently in French- and English-language editions in England, not to mention its translations into Polish, Russian, Swedish, Italian, and Greek.[5]

Mme Leprince de Beaumont's book is known today principally because it houses her enduringly famous version of "Beauty and the Beast,"[6] but her compendious book of readings also supplied European girls of the middle and upper classes with moralized versions of French fairy tales taken from the works of earlier French fairy tale tellers such as Charles Perrault (1628–1703), Mme d'Aulnoy 1650/51–1705), and Gabrielle Suzanne de Villeneuve (1685–1755), her source for "Beauty and the Beast." For her young girl readers she carefully edited all of the tales she chose for her book, which was read in their newly didacticized forms throughout Europe by youngsters of the educated classes. It is thus Mme Leprince's book that provided an impulse for some of the earliest fairy tale translations from French into other European languages and that partly accounts for the swift spread of late seventeenth- and early eighteenth-century French fairy tales throughout Europe.[7]

Below, and before, the many printings of Mme Leprince de Beaumont's books for middle-, upper-middle-, and upper-class girls, there is again a mixed layer of books of fairy tales with titles as various as *New Fairy Tales* (Nouveaux Contes de Fées), *Entertaining Days, dedicated to the King* (Les Journées amusantes dédiées au Roy), and *Little Evening Repasts* (Les Petits Soupers). In the six or seven years before and after 1700, however, a dense layer of fairy tales comes to light.[8] In this stratum appear two 4–volume editions of *contes de fées* (fairy tales and tales about fairies) by Mme d'Aulnoy and two more multi-volume ones by Mme de Murat, as well as a host of books by authors whose names are known only to dedicated scholars. Here, too, are the Paris printings of Charles Perrault's *Histories, or Tales of Past Times* (Histoires, ou Contes du temps passé), and an Amsterdam pirating of it a few months later. Intermixed are volumes that declare their novelty with ones that claim the fairy tyranny to have been destroyed.

The titles of some of the tales in the immediate pre- and post-1700 books—such as "Sleeping Beauty," "Cinderella," and "Puss in Boots"—are familiar to most contemporary readers. Other titles are alien to modern ears, although their content is often well known. Mlle Lhéritier's "Ricdin-Ricdon" tells a Rumpelstiltskin story; her "Enchantments of Eloquence" has the same general plot as Perrault's "Diamonds and Toads" (also known as "The Fairies"), in which jewels issue from a good daughter's mouth, while toads leap over and serpents slither past her bad stepsister's lips. Mlle Lhéritier's "Discreet Princess" and her very indiscreet sisters have been in English as "Finette" as long as Perrault's own tales have been (and were long thought to have been one of his own creations). Charlotte Rose de la Force's "Persinette" is none other than the beloved "Rapunzel."

ITALIAN BOOKS AND FRENCH FAIRY TALES

Perrault got most of his tales from Italian books, just as his niece Mlle Lhéritier (1664–1734), and the *conteuse* Mme d'Aulnoy and her many successors took motifs, episodes, and sometimes entire plots from those same foreign sources. They did so circum-spectly, however, for the taste for genteel seemliness in 1690s Paris was very different from the love of raucous humor in 1630s Naples or 1550s Venice. In using tales from south of the Alps, French fairy tale tellers had to tame their boisterous Italian pred-ecessors. This chapter argues that Charles Perrault and his niece Marie-Jeanne Lhéritier did not get their stories from French peasants or illiterate folk nursemaids. Instead, it argues that the plots of the majority of French fairy tales from the 1690s came from Italians, specifically, from two Italian books. It is an argu-ment for which the metaphor of archaeology is both useful and telling and which helps in producing an account of French fairy tales that reflects the layered nature of their origins.

The first French-authored fairy tale that corresponds to the definition for fairy tales worked out in chapter 1 appeared in 1694, four years after Mme d'Aulnoy's tale about fairyland, "The Island of Happiness" (L'Ile de la Félicité). In that year Charles Perrault produced one of those complex verse creations that flowed so effortlessly from his pen. He called it "Peau d'Asne. Conte." (Donkeyskin. A Tale.). Dedicated to the Marquise de Lambert, a woman who at that time was in the process of legally regaining the wealth to which she was entitled by birth and mar-riage, it detailed the travails of a heroine who had suffered the loss of her rightful goods and property. Dedicating this tale to her was therefore altogether appropriate, since Perrault's "Donkeyskin," was also a tale of a young woman's deprivation followed by a rightful restoration to her heritage.

I use the verb "compose" intentionally in dicussing the creation of "Donkeyskin." Just as a chef assembles a *salade composé* from existing ingredients, so too did Perrault take constituent elements for his "Donkeyskin" from books by two earlier creators of fairy tale and fairy tale-like stories.[9] The first was the seventeenth-century Neapolitan Giambattista Basile (c.1585–1632), who wrote *Lo cunto de li cunti* (The Tale of the Tales, in 5 parts, 1634–1636); the second, the sixteenth-century Venetian Giovan Francesco Straparola (c.1485–c.1557), author of *Le Piacevoli Notti* (Pleasant Nights in 2 vols. 1551, 1553). As we dig more deeply into the fairy tale past, we will encounter these two again, but I touch on their works now, because their presence in the first fairy tale composed by a French author tells us something important about the history of European fairy tales.

In Perrault's day, amusing stories with some magic in them had a generic name, "donkeyskin stories" or *contes de peau d'asne*, whether or not there actually was a donkeyskin in their plot. It was just like Charles Perrault to have made a terminological joke out of his first effort at writing a fairy tale. He meant to write a *donkeyskin* tale, a nonrational tale adorned with magic, and so he composed a fiction about just that, a donkeyskin.

Perrault loved this kind of humor and was very clever at it. He was also a skilled reformulator, attested to by the large proportion of his works that consisted of literary commentaries upon or reworkings of existing published works. Therefore it is no surprise when we see his first fairy tale following that familiar pattern, a composition of elements taken directly from published tales by Basile and Straparola. Basile's donkeyskin tale was raunchily suggestive and Straparola's stylistically rough, whereas Perrault's writing was sexually modest, socially decent, and, in the end, highly moral. His contribution to the history of the tale as

Basile, and before him Straparola, had told it was a decorous seemliness, and it resulted in the following tale:

> There was once a mighty prince for whom a marvelous donkey provided unending wealth by excreting gold. When the king's charming and beautiful wife fell ill and lay dying, she made him promise that he would re-marry, but only someone wiser and more beautiful than she. After her death the king searched for months, and then fell violently in love with his wise and beautiful daughter.
>
> The terrified princess sought help and advice from her fairy godmother (*maraine*), who advised her to put her father off with impossible requirements, such as a dress the color of weather.[10] He provided it, as he also did when she required a second one the color of the moon, and a third, the color of the sun. He also gave her the skin of his gold-producing donkey, even though granting that wish destroyed the very source of his immense wealth. The king's acquiescence to every one of his daughter's demands left her no alternative but flight, and so she fled her home to escape his incestuous desire. In disguise, she made her way to a distant kingdom where she took work in the kitchen of a great farm. Behind locked doors on Sundays, however, she put on her exquisite gowns.
>
> One day the princely owner of the farm paid it a visit. Seeing him from afar and not knowing who he was, Princess Donkeyskin developed tender feelings for him. For his part, when he caught sight of her in her extraordinary dress, he fell deeply in love with *her*. The lovesick prince stopped eating, declaring that he'd take food only from the hand of the girl he'd been told was called Donkeyskin. Knowing this, the disguised princess prepared a

fine cake, into which she dropped her ring. When the prince found it and declared he would marry whomever the ring fit, girls all over the kingdom, from duchesses to servingmaids pared (or puffed) their fingers to fit it. In the end only the lowly Donkeyskin's finger perfectly fit the ring.

To the wedding came all manner of guests, including Donkeyskin's own father. The passage of time had purified him of his criminal passion. *[This is the seemly conclusion that Perrault added.]* The princely bridegroom was, of course, delighted to learn that his bride was not a scullery maid, but the gloriously virtuous scion of an illustrious royal family.

Many tales of consummated incestuous desire predated this one. In the early medieval *King Apollonius of Tyre* the king of Antioch kept his beautiful daughter in thrall, and in the end they both died in a dramatic lightening strike. Other instances of incest can be found in the middle ages, because plenty of medieval narratives had fathers and uncles molesting—or trying to molest—daughters and nieces, some of whom subsequently, and consequently, became saints. The attempted incest in Perrault's "Donkeyskin" differed fundamentally, however, because it was not only unsuccessful, but also deeply repented.

Donkeys and their skins have a long and independent existence in European literature. In antiquity Apuleius's Latin *Golden Ass* had a story in which, at one point, a donkeyskin cloaked a frightened girl to whom a crone was telling the story of "Cupid and Psyche." Well schooled in the classics, Perrault would surely have known that tale. He may also have known Bonaventure des Périers's sixteenth-century story about a girl whose father dressed her in a donkeyskin to drive off a suitor. A storyline like Perrault's, with imminent incest expelling the heroine from her royal eminence into a servile station, however, occurs in two particularly interesting places before Perrault put pen to paper: the first was *Les facetieux nuictz* (The Pleasant Nights) of Jean François Straparole, none other than our Venetian friend Giovan Francesco Straparola. His little book had at least sixteen reprintings in France, several of them in Paris, and to judge from the elaborate binding of some extant copies, it was a prized book. If this isn't sufficient evidence to prove the likely presence of Straparola's stories in Paris, and in particular, in Perrault's own study, then one final piece of information should be satisfactorily conclusive. Mme de Murat (1670–1716), a contemporary of Perrault's, claimed in the *Avertissement* of her *Sublime and Allegorical Stories* (Histoires sublimes et allégoriques, 1699) that everybody, including herself, was taking their stories from "Straparole."[11]

The story line of Perrault's "Donkeyskin" had also appeared in Giambattista Basile's *Tale of the Tales*, popularly called *The Pentamerone*.[12] His book is generally thought to have been unknown in seventeenth-century France, but its influence is so widely apparent that we must question that assumption. In 2007 Suzanne Magnanini's brilliant literary detective work placed one or more copies of Basile's recently published Neapolitan-dialect *Tale of the Tales* in Paris within inches of Perrault at the French Academy, where he spent several days every week and from which location he could easily have carried it home.[13]

So far every argument about Perrault's indebtedness to his Italian predecessors has been based on context, that is, on historical evidence outside the texts of the tales in question. In terms of textual analysis, however, one need only lay the three texts for the donkeyskin tales—Perrault's, Basile's, and Straparola's—side by side to justify using the verb "compose" in the sense of putting together existing elements. Three identifiable components of Perrault's tale derive neither from Straparola nor from Basile, and not one of these three reflects peasant experience. Instead, each expresses a refined humor typical of Perrault's writings as a whole:

1. an exiled princess privately dressing up on Sundays for her own pleasure;
2. a king inspecting his menagerie at the farm where the disguised princess served as a scullery maid;
3. and ladies of the kingdom paring their fingers to make them fit the ring the king had found in his *gateau*.

The last words of Perrault's "Donkeyskin" are these:

> Donkeyskin's story is hard to believe,
> But as long as the world has children,
>   Mothers, and grandmothers,
>   People will remember her.

Not nursemaids, but mothers and grandmothers, inhabit this verse. Nowhere does Perrault mention a nursemaid, but in the history of this tale a nursemaid's presence has always been assumed and asserted. In a revised history of European fairy tales, illiterate nursemaid sources don't exist (although there's plenty of room for household help from Paris who might have read a copy of *Les Facetieux Nuictz!*).

In the next year, 1695, two other works that are crucial for a new history of European fairy tales appeared in print. One, *L'Œuvres Meslées*, was by Marie-Jeanne Lhéritier de Villandon, Perrault's then thirty-one-year old niece. Although textual comparisons demonstrate conclusively that Mlle Lhéritier took the plots for the tales in *L'Œuvres Meslées* from published Italian precursors, she had her own theories about the history of these stories. In her view, they were literary survivals from the writings of medieval troubadors.[14] However, neither of her first two fairy tales come from any known troubadour writings; instead we find the plots of both tales in Basile's collection.[15] The first, "The Enchantments of Eloquence" (Les Enchantements d'éloquence), was a rise fairy tale; the second, "The Discreet Princess, or the Adventures of Finette" (L'Adroite Princesse, ou les aventures de

Finette) was a typical morality tale into which she worked magical elements.[16] Ten years later Mlle Lhéritier composed a third, "Ricdin-Ricdon," another rise tale.[17] This one reworked Basile's "The Seven Little Pork Rinds" (Le sette Cotennine), which told, at great length, a "Rumpelstiltskin" kind of story.

In addition to "The Enchantments of Eloquence" and "The Discreet Princess," Mlle Lhéritier had—in 1695—reworked another tale that appeared both in Straparola's collection and in Basile's. She had turned to Straparola's version of an enduringly popular medieval crossdressing tale, "Costanzo-Costanza," for the immediate plot of her "Marmoisan." Straparola's tale details the experiences of a princess who made her way in the world by dressing as a man and entering the service of a foreign king. Alas for her, the king's lascivious consort fell in love with Costanza-Costanzo and tried to seduce the new, attractive, and apparently male, courtier. When she failed, she set an impossible task, to capture a satyr, which Costanza-Costanzo carried out successfully. Through the satyr the king learned that Costanza-Costanzo was a woman and that his wife's handmaids were crossdressed men, and so he executed the queen and married the crossdressing heroine Costanza.

Basile, too, produced a bawdy crossdressing tale, "The Three Crowns" (Day 4, Story 6), about a princess who masqueraded as a merchant at a distant royal court. There the queen fell in love with him/her, and when rebuffed, brought (unsustainable!) charges that "he" had sexually assaulted her. When the truth came out, the king drowned his wife and, as in Straparola's tale, married the crossdressing heroine.[18] Basile's tales bore more resemblance to dramas of the previous century that made low comedy out of determining the sex of a confusingly disguised protagonist than they did to a fairy tale plot.

From this unmannerly Italian material Mlle Lhéritier composed not a fairy tale, but a novella, whose title—"Marmoisin, or the Innocent Deception" (Marmoisan, ou l'innocente tromperie)—vigorously protested its heroine's innocence. We learn a lot about *what* Mlle Lhéritier considered "innocent" from her story. *Who* was indecorous and *who* spoke bawdily seems to have counted far more than *what* was actually done or said. For instance, the heroine's wastrel twin brother had been cuckolding a king, for which he was run through.[19] Mlle Lhéritier retained his amoral escapades as a foil for his twin sister's staunch virtue. Similarly, when the sister took her brother's place at court and mixed with rowdy courtiers, their rough conversation, rude stories, and sexual grossness allowed Mlle Lhéritier to have her heroine blush and, hence, signal an innate and praiseworthy modesty.[20]

In Mlle Lhéritier's "Marmoisan," a truly male prince found himself unaccountably and deeply drawn to an ostensibly male companion. When suspicions were raised that the "he" for whom he felt a deep inclination was really a "she," the prince fervently hoped they were right. Mlle Lhéritier even had the heroine herself express a socially correct attitude by occasionally wishing to wear women's clothes again.[21] Indeed, at the end, she returned to her female self, and as Léonore, married the prince and lived many happy years with her royal husband. This is Mlle Lhéritier's 1695 taming of an Italian tale.[22]

In 1695 Perrault was busy preparing a small manuscript collection of tales for Louis XIV's nineteen-year-old niece, Élisabeth-Charlotte d'Orléans (1676–1744). He had written four tales—"Sleeping Beauty" (La belle au bois dormant), "Little Red Riding Hood" (Le petit chaperon rouge), "Bluebeard" (La Barbe bleüe), and "Puss in Boots" (Le maistre Chat). The fifth tale he composed for Élisabeth-Charlotte was "The Fairies" (Les Fées).

The order in which the five tales of Perrault's collection appear is in itself interesting, perhaps revealing. The first seems to be based on Basile's "Sun, Moon, and Talia" (Sole, Luna e Talia). The second and third tales—"Red Riding Hood" and "Blue Beard"—are both morality tales with no known precursors in European literary history, and there is much that points to Perrault's having written them himself. The fourth tale comes straight from Straparola's "Puss in Boots" tale "Costantino Fortunato," while Perrault's fifth tale, "The Fairies," is one that his niece had reworked from Basile's "Two Little Pizzas" as "The Enchantments of Eloquence." There is much in the content and style of Perrault's "Fairies" that suggests he knew Mlle Lhéritier's "Enchantments of Eloquence," as well as Basile's two tales, "The Three Fairies" (Le tre fate) and "The Two Little Pizzas" (Le due pizzette). Above all, the fact that Perrault placed his "Fairies" last suggests that it was the last tale he composed and furthermore that he composed it *after* Mlle Lhéritier had composed her "Enchantments."[23] Neither Perrault nor Mlle Lhéritier wrote any more fairy tales in 1695, which suggests that there was no further need or immediate impetus for doing so at that moment.

Perrault's reworking, a classic version of the Good Sister–Bad Sister fairy tale type, became known in English as "Diamonds and Toads," a tale that perfectly melded morality and magic. It also forged the reigning model for modern morality tales, in which magic rewards good behavior.

If Perrault so frequently reworked existing narratives, then a question arises about Mlle Lhéritier's "Marmoisan." It remained her story alone, but that said, something deeply fascinating and relevant emerges from Basile's version of that tale. To explain why a tale that Perrault did *not* take up and refashion can be as revealing as one that he did, we need to look again at the manuscript collection of tales for Élisabeth-Charlotte d'Orléans. In Perrault's 1695 manuscript collection for her, one of the tales with no known precursor, "Blue Beard," betrays his knowledge of the Basile precursor story that Mlle Lhéritier had fashioned into "Marmoisan." It is a knowledge that emerges from a dialogue between an ogress and a princess keeping house for her:

> Here are the keys of the house, over which you shall have full sway and dominion. I make only one reservation: on no account must you open the last room, to which this key belongs; if you did . . . (4:6).[24]

Those words come from Basile's "Three Crowns" (Le tre corone). Basile's heroine is, of course, overcome by "curiosity" and she opens the door, behind which she finds three girls.[25] This would later become none other than the pivotal moment in Perrault's "Blue Beard" tale. Its ancestry has long been alleged to lie in a folk memory of earlier centuries' infamous mass murderers. But "Blue Beard's" origins lie closer to hand, for if Perrault rejected the rest of Basile's verbally suggestive "Three Crowns," he seized upon just this material to construct a warning morality tale of his own making.

A common objection to Perrault's having used a copy of Basile's tales as a source for his own is the assumption that Basile's Neapolitan dialect is now and would then have been too difficult for Perrault to understand. Seventeenth-century usage, as Basile incorporated it into the *Pentamerone*, is opaque to most modern readers, but the Neapolitan phrases about keys and a forbidden room are less so, and as Nancy Canepa, the foremost American Basile scholar notes, "the general Italian public had a passing familiarity with Neapolitan" because of its use in theater and the *commedia dell'arte*.[26] Consider the following text:

> . . . perzò eccote le chiave de le cammare e singhe
> domene e domenanzio. Sulo me reservo na cosa: che non
> vuoglie aprire 'n cunto nesciuno l'utema cammara, dove
> va bona sta chiave, che me farrisse saglire buono la
> mostarda a lo naso . . .[27]

At first glance this text puzzles an English, or perhaps even a modern French reader. But consider the possibility that a verbal adept like Perrault would have recognized not only the text's threatening mode but would also have understood a central phrase such as the keys of the chamber. Although Perrault was well-schooled in Latin—he would publish his translation of Faerno's Latin *Fabulae* (*Fables*) in 1697—he needed but little Latin skill to understand the substance of Basile's language.

Basile's Neapolitan keys (*chiave*) and the Latin *claves*, the modern Italian *chiavi* and the modern French *clefs*. The Neapolitan chambers (*cammare*) of which the last is forbidden are modern Italian *camere* and the modern French *chambres*. It could hardly have been difficult for Perrault to understand Basile's "*non aprire*" (don't open), "*per nessuna ragione*" (for any reason), "*l'ultima camera*" (the last room), "*questa chiave*" (this key), or even "*il sangue*" (blood).[28] And if Charles Perrault had any problems understanding Basile's text, he could have asked his brother Pierre who was at ease in Italian.[29]

Basile's restoration fairy tale flowed forward in its magic mode as its heroine, driven on by her curiosity to know what was in the forbidden chamber ("*la curiosità de vedere . . .*"), found three princesses enchanted by a fairy. In his "Blue-Beard" Perrault transformed Basile's immobilized women into female victims of a cruel and blue-bearded husband and made them crucial elements for a shocking morality about curiosity causing women's downfall.

Basile had had a way with stories. Some call it fresh, some charming. Basile's fifty rough and tumble stories (forty-nine tales set within a frame tale that was itself a tale) were certainly outrageous and needed taming before they could enter polite society. In taming those tales Perrault created Europe's best-known fairy tales. For instance, nearly everyone knows Perrault's "Cinderella" story, which Walt Disney brought into the imaginations of the world's filmgoing children. Cheap and popular American print versions describe its heroine just as Perrault created her: sleeping on straw, sitting among the cinders, but patient, meek, and obliging, she irons her haughty stepsisters' undergarments, neatens their ruffles, advises them about ball gowns, and combs their hair. A fairy godmother helps her get to a ball, where she arrives in glory and dances with a prince who promptly falls in love with her. At a second ball Cinderella enjoys herself so much that she stays too long and has to flee as the clock strikes twelve, dropping one of her glass slippers in her haste. The prince searches the kingdom for the girl whom the slipper fits, until Cinderella offers her foot and produces the matching slipper. Proving her unending goodness, Perrault's heroine forgives her wicked stepsisters, and after her own wedding to the prince, gives them palace apartments and marries them to great nobles.

Basile's cinder-heroine is a world away. Her name, also the story's title, "The Cinderella Cat" (La Gatta Cenerentola), prepares us for the hiss and the scratch that follow: The widowed father of Basile's Cinderella took a perfect harridan as his second wife, a woman who made our heroine's life such a misery that little Cinderella Cat complained to her governess. Seeing opportunity, the governess told Cinderella to slam a trunk lid onto her stepmother's neck to be quit of her for good and all, and then to beg her father to take her (the governess) as his new wife, promising that she would then give Cinderella the best of everything. And thus it happened. It was as a murderess that Basile's Cinderella Cat began her ascent to the throne.

Perrault's "Sleeping Beauty" is nearly as much a part of contemporary narrative culture as is "Cinderella." The source of his tale was a Basilean slumbering heroine who was visited by a passing king who had sex with her, with the result that—nine months later and still-sleeping—she gave birth to twins. Only when one of her babies mistakenly sucked on her fingertip and pulled out the sleep-causing splinter did she awaken, amazed at the infant companions she found beside her on the bed. The tale played out with the king's continuing bigamy, an attempted murder, and a comic striptease, after which the bigamous king set everything right. Basile had not invented this tale, but he maintained the essential elements and the spirit of a much longer and far bawdier version—already a few centuries old when Basile took it up—in his reworking.

Perrault's version of "Sleeping Beauty" harnessed Basile's plot but curbed its sexuality by putting a chaplain in the princess's bedchamber to marry the newly awakened heroine and her prince before any unlicensed monkey business could begin. Then he coyly noted that the two slept but little that night. The bride, Perrault observed, was well rested from her century-long slumber; he didn't try to account for the prince's wakefulness.

For the fourth of his five tales in the 1695 manuscript for Élisabeth-Charlotte, Perrault reworked Straparola's "Costantino Fortunato." He scrubbed off its hero's filth, polished his boorish manners, made Straparola's fairy-godmother graymalkin into a self-assured tom, and out came his famous "Puss in Boots."

Perrault adopted and adapted the details of Straparola's plot. More importantly, however, he found in Straparola's stripped-down style a perfect textual model for his project of creating contemporary French tales in a modern mode. This was central to his literary and ethical position in the Battle of the Ancients and the Moderns, in which he was embroiled at the same time that he was composing his fairy tales. We may understand Straparola's role in Perrault's tales as having introduced a folk tone (as opposed to the high literary level of his previously published "Griselidis," "Peau d'Asne," and "The Three Ridicuous Wishes") among France's earliest fairy tales. Basile's role in the history of European fairy tales differed. Although he had used folk characters, had frequently referred to street life and activities, and had written in Neapolitan dialect, his ornate Baroque literary style was anything but folk in nature. Together, however, Straparola's tone added to Basile's plots and motifs provided models for Perrault's composition of modern French stories. Perrault meant the resultant newly composed stories to demonstrate the superiority of modern tales and their morals over those of the ancients.

Perrault's contemporaries, Madame d'Aulnoy and Madame de Murat, also used Straparola stories as a basis for many of their fairy tale creations. Their borrowings of Straparola plots led to different results, however, because they both wrote in the more elaborate prose style of earlier seventeenth-century précieuse French novels. Let us set Straparola's "Pierre insensé" (as "Pietro Pazzo" had been translated into French) next to Mme d'Aulnoy's "The Dolphin / Dauphin" (Le Dauphin) in order to examine the telling difference between what was acceptable in a 1550s Venetian hero in a rise fairy tale vs. what Mme d'Aulnoy put into a 1690s Parisian restoration fairy tale. Straparola's principal male figure had been a filthy-mouthed, lazy, dirt-encrusted anti-hero who was mean to his mother. Consistent with his uncouth manners, he cursed a ten-year-old princess living across the street and coarsely wished her pregnant. In marvelous contrast to his boorish father was the baby boy of surpassing beauty that the now eleven-year-old princess bore nine months later. That birth brought down her father's wrath, so that eventually she, its father the street urchin Pietro, and the baby were all stuffed into a wine cask and thrown into the sea. Magic, however, saved them and led to a family reconciliation and a happy ending.

Straparola's story had a share of phallic imagery drawn from medieval fabliaux. His rough and ready plot that raised an urban urchin from the gutter to a palace presumably suited the taste of the part of his urban readership that was rough and ready. Straparola's book sold well in Venice, and it sold just as well in late sixteenth- and early seventeenth-century France.[30] But its unwashed hero was *un*acceptable to late seventeenth-century French readers in Madame d'Aulnoy's circle, who evidently shared the refined sensibilities of Charles Perrault's friends and colleagues. Hence, Mme d'Aulnoy royalized Straparola's tuna into a dolphin, whose French translation *dauphin* also designated the heir to the French throne. The "dauphin" then replaced stupid Pierre in the title of her story. Her hero was not a gormless fool like Straparola's, but a royal prince whose only fault was his homeliness. Ridiculed by the courtiers of the princess he loved, he found a way to approach her intimately by becoming a bird named Bébé, whom she cosseted and let sleep in her room at night, a bird the idea for which Mme d'Aulnoy may well taken from one of Basile's metaphors in his telling of the tale.[31] The magical dolphin (*dauphin*) who had brought all this about had decorously forbidden Bébé to sleep with the princess before they were properly married, which necessitated a ceremony that the princess thought a sham, but that licensed the hero to transform himself at night from feathered friend into his natural, manly form. In this manner, and ever so delicately, he impregnated the princess while she slept.

Mme d'Aulnoy complicated her "Dauphin" story and altered its genre by introducing fairyland and the enmity of a malign fairy named Grognette, which considerably extended the story's plot. Nonetheless, her text contained unmistakeable references to Straparola's text.[32] Mme d'Aulnoy also made it clear that she had improved on Straparola's plot by having her princess announce that she was sixteen, an age far more appropriate for childbearing than Straparola's eleven, and as such, an age that hints that Mme d'Aulnoy's readers already knew that Straparola's princess had been criminally underage for either marriage or motherhood.

Mme d'Aulnoy's borrowings weren't limited to Straparola. For a colorful toad and serpent imagery to accompany her wicked fairy, Mme d'Aulnoy unabashedly drew on Perrault's "Fairies," which had appeared in print a few months before her own volume did.[33]

Mme d'Aulnoy's "Dauphin" story is five times as long as the translation of Straparola's tale, "Pierre insensé" in its many sixteenth- and seventeenth-century French printings. Her story wasn't lengthened by an increased amount of action but by her characters' lengthy discussions of their emotions at every stage in the plot's development. This discursive aspect became characteristic of many other stories composed by late seventeenth-century women writers of fairy tales, whose principle source was similarly Straparola.

Just as Basile had provided one plot and several motifs for Perrault, Charlotte Rose de la Force's "Persinette" (1697) also drew

on Basile, in particular on his "Petrosinella" (Day 2, Story 1). Her
"Persinette," which was published soon after both Perrault and
Lhéritier had turned to Basile, raises an interesting question:
Might all three writers have shared a single book? Might Mme
d'Aulnoy similarly have had access to this rare book?

In sharp contrast, later French fairy tale writers ceased to
draw directly on Basile's *oeuvre*. The inability, or failure, or disin-
clination to do so, suggests a range of explanations. Perhaps they
had access to a copy of the *Pentamerone* but being perhaps less
schooled in Latin and perhaps not knowing Italian, could not
read its Neapolitan dialect. Alternatively, they may not have
had any access to a copy of Basile's tales at all. In its turn, this
possibility raises several further questions.

1. What happened to the copy of Basile's tales that Perrault and Mlle Lhéritier seem so surely to have used?
2. If there were other copies of *The Pentamerone* in Paris,
   even if only a few, why did they not survive in the
   Royal Library (now the Bibliothèque nationale) or in
   the Arsenal (home to so many seventeenth-century
   books)?
3. Did the influence in Louis XIV's court of Mme de
   Maintenon's piety extend to library shelves?
4. Or was it the Catholic Index of forbidden books that
   led to the *Pentamerone*'s absence from French library
   holdings? If that is the case, it should be archivally
   verifiable.

Whatever the reason for the absence of seventeenth-century
copies of Basile's *Pentamerone* from French libraries, the fact that
the emergence of story content from Basile's collection clusters
around a small group of later seventeenth-century French
authors, and the fact that it appears within a very few years following 1694 points towards several significant conclusions:

1. Mlle Lhéritier, Charles Perrault, Mlle de la Force and perhaps Mme d'Aulnoy shared a common source.
2. Later authors did not have access to the common source used by Mlle Lhéritier, Perrault, Mlle de la Force, and perhaps Mme d'Aulnoy.
3. The source turned to by the four authors could not have been the French peasantry, the content of whose oral tradition—if it had existed—would have been equally available to later authors and would have emerged among their tales as well.
4. Therefore, the common sources used by the authors in question—Mlle Lhéritier, Perrault, d'Aulnoy, and de la Force—was one to which they had exclusive access.
5. That kind of limited and exclusive source was in all likelihood a single copy of Basile's *Pentamerone*.

Inevitably, people want to know who was first to newly compose fairy tales in France. Was it Charles Perrault? Or was it Mlle Lhéritier? No reliable data tell us which came first, the stories of Mlle Lhéritier's book with its 1695 *privilège* or those of the 1695 manuscript of her uncle Charles Perrault. I've examined Lhéritier's and Perrault's tales of the good and bad sisters and their respective magical rewards and curses. I've compared them with each other and with the two Basile tales that preceded them. And I've concluded that Perrault may well have had his niece's tale as well as Basile's two tales in front of him when he composed "The Fairies."[34] But before the tales that both Charles Perrault and Mlle Lhéritier composed in 1695, there was Perrault's 1694 "Donkeyskin," which amalgamated elements from Straparola as well as from Basile into a story with an altered plot and changed motivations. It appears most likely that Perrault first made use of Straparola's and Basile's tale collections, and that Mlle Lhéritier followed so closely in his footsteps that their writings affected each other in 1695 and 1696.

In the next few years, French-authored fairy tales by Perrault, Mlle Lhéritier, Mlle de la Force, Mme d'Aulnoy, and Mme de Murat continued to borrow from Basile or Straparola, and sometimes from both. The next chapter will discuss Straparola and Basile themselves, the two foundational European shapers of fairy tales. Straparola created the form. Basile provided much of the content that later authors adopted. Together, one after the other, they created the basis for Europe's fairy tale tradition.

THE TWO INVENTORS
OF FAIRY TALE TRADITION

Giambattista Basile (1634–1636) and
Giovan Francesco Straparola (1551, 1553)

THEORETICAL RECAPITULATION

Chapter 2 outlined two very different histories of the Grimms' tales. By showing that France provided Germany with its fairy tale tradition, and by concluding that folk knowledge of fairy tales followed upon their book distribution, chapter 2 supported a revision of the history of fairy tales. Chapter 3 focused on late seventeenth-century French authors—Perrault, Mlle Lhéritier, and Mme d'Aulnoy, along with Mme de Murat and Mlle de la Force—and examined those writers' adoptions of plots from two Italian precursors, Giambattista Basile and Giovan Francesco Straparola. It also described the strategies of adaptation that French authors used to tame their Italian forebears' brutish stories. In these chapters the genre differences between tales about fairyland and fairy tales, first outlined in chapter 1, loom large. So, too, do distinctions between restoration and rise fairy tales.

It's reasonable to expect more variation among fairy tale plots than the two basic ones discussed here, that is, restoration and rise fairy tales. That is, in fact, the case, when a rise fairy tale is lengthened by adding on a second, restoration fairy tale plot: a poor hero or heroine can achieve a happy ending by marrying into royal ranks, after which treachery plunges the now-royal hero (usually it is the hero rather than the heroine who experiences betrayal at this point) into a new round of suffering, from which magic eventually restores him to his now-rightful royal position. A second restoration plot can also be knit onto the ending of a restoration fairy tale.

Even though a simple restoration or rise fairy tale can be lengthened by adding a restoration sequence, the individual restoration and rise plot units can still be discerned. The terms "restoration" and "rise" shouldn't be considered as mechanically exact descriptions of every existing fairy tale that ends happily with a wedding brought about by magic. Instead, "restoration" and "rise" fairy tale plot lines describe a series of events in a fairy tale plot.

The markers that distinguish fairy tales from tales about fairyland are not plot- and character-based (poor vs. royal protagonists who suffer tasks and trials), but are paradigmatic in nature. To recapitulate the description in chapter 1 once again, fairy tales play out in the world of human beings, into which magical forces intrude, but tales about fairies and fairyland exist on two planes (on a human plane and on an otherworldly plane where different natural laws obtain), back and forth between which a fairy tale hero or heroine moves.

Using markers to identify individual tales as tales about fairies and fairyland on the one hand, and as restoration and rise fairy tales on the other hand, refines the examination and comparison of individual fairy tales within Europe's immense corpus in a systematic and reliable manner. I've repeated the information here, because it is easy—when using a new set of terms—to stray from an author's intended definitions, and as a whole the argument of this book grows out of the distinctions outlined here.

TRADITIONAL TALE COLLECTIONS

In the 1620s, when Basile is thought to have composed the individual stories of the fifty-story *Lo cunto de li cunti* (The Tale of the Tales), now widely known as the *Pentamerone*, tale collections were a centuries-old and well-established literary genre. In form, a tale collection comprises a group of stories—tens or scores of them. Typically, authors borrowed stories from earlier tale collections, their own "authorship" consisting of updating a tale's language or freshening up its plot. This an author might do by altering a tale's style and vocabulary or by inserting new and timely details, such as references to personages known to the book's potential readers or mentionings of places familiar to those readers.

In terms of their organization, tale collections had a conventional form. Stories were not simply thrown together helter skelter, but were set within an overarching framing narrative, within which an author contrived to have each tale told by a named narrator. This narrator might be a wholly fictitious and newly invented person or might bear the name of and exemplify characteristics of a known historical personage. In creating a group of narrators, tale collection authors tried to create a sense of verisimilitude by making it seem likely that the particular group of people shown in the (fictitious) frame tale had (really) gathered and told stories. If a frame tale's storytellers were obviously fictional, then an author's project was to create the illusion that the assembled narrators could have gathered together. An author's effort to foster believability grew out of a powerful literary convention that drove late medieval and early modern novellas, namely, the notion that both the tellings and the plots did, or could well have, taken place. Hence, a tale collection author routinely implied that the gathering described in a frame tale had taken place at a specific time and place. Medieval and early modern readers knew the conventions of their age, but modern readers who aren't schooled in theories of verisimilitude can easily mistake fictive frame tale situations, such as Straparola's gathering on the island of Murano or Basile's in Naples, for real ones.[1]

A collection's framing tale was itself subject to literary conventions about the storytelling characters and the occasion for their storytelling. Stories in continental European tale collections were generally told by a small group of highborn or noble narrators, each of whom represented an ideal of beauty or social accomplishment. Continental European (as opposed to English) frame tales typically depicted a group fleeing from, and successfully escaping, a common danger, such as disastrous weather, epidemic disease. or political unrest. In flight from natural or man-made cataclysms, the frame tale's ideal narrators remained together for a set period—seven, ten, thirteen days—and amused themselves in their isolation by telling each other stories. Characteristically, the storytellers' location was remote from the danger that threatened them—on a mountain high above the flood, in the country far from urban plague, or on an island safe from political turmoil.[2]

A tale collection was conciously literary, or was meant to be so. Related to and dependent on its anticipated readership, its language was consequently Latin for educated priests, government officials, and scholars, while for general lay readers it was usually in the local spoken language, such as Italian or French. In style it aimed high. The exemplar for all tale collections from the fourteenth century onward was Giovanni Boccaccio's *Decameron* (1353), plots for whose stories came from sources as various as bawdy fabliaux, pious sermon tales, publicly performed popular tale cycles, and ancient myth.[3]

Like authors before and after him, Boccaccio reworked existing stories, retelling them masterfully.[4] He set a lofty tone at the outset by enunciating a high ideal: "Human it is to have compassion for the afflicted."[5] In particular, he offered his collection "for the succor and solace" of a particular afflicted group, "ladies in love" (1:5). The stories themselves, he claimed in an age-old literary trope, had been told by others, in this case "by an honorable company of seven ladies and three young men." Their stories were—in the terms of his day—morally exemplary, because readers would find "useful counsel" about what behavior to avoid and what acts to emulate (1:5).

Boccaccio's seven ladies were young—all between 18 and 28—and wealthy. In addition, "each was discreet and of noble blood, fair of favor and well mannered and of gracious bearing" (1:17). For manly guidance, the seven women took along three "gracious and well bred" (1:21) young men, and on the following "Wednesday" (1:22)—a precise date that promoted verisimilitude—they set out together for a country estate two short miles from Florence. It was "situated on a little hill, somewhat withdrawn on every side from our main roads and full of various shrubs and plants, all green of leafage and pleasant to behold. On the summit of this hill was a palace . . . with lawns and grassplots . . . and marvelous gardens and wells of very cold water and cellars full of the finest wines" (1:23). Boccaccio's narrators were ideal, their surroundings equally so.[6]

GIAMBATTISTA BASILE: *LO CUNTO DE LI CUNTI*

When Giambattista Basile created *his* tale collection, he inverted every one of Boccaccio's well-known ideals. His opening statements stressed not the nobility of human compassion, but a frame tale scene that mocked suffering. In Basile's frame tale, human beings, their bodies, and their emotions became a stage for low comedy. Even royalty was drawn into that degrading scene. The overarching frame tale begins with Princess Zoza who cannot, or does not, laugh, and whose father tries everything to make her do so. Finally, the king sets up a fountain spouting oil, which brings about laughter-inducing comedy, when an old woman laboriously sops up oil for her jug. A rude boy breaks her jug, and in anger she exposes herself to him. The princess finally laughs, but her mirth brings down the crone's curse that the only husband she will ever have is Prince Tadeo of the Round Field, whom she must first disenchant by filling a jug with her tears within three days. The princess is robbed of the prince by a slave girl, who makes off with the nearly filled jug and finishes the job, thus gaining the prince for herself. Nine months later the princess, with the aid of three fairies' gifts, gains admittance to the prince's castle where everyone is awaiting the birth of the false bride's child. There Princess Zoza excites a desire for stories in the pregnant woman, and Prince Tadeo gathers ten repellent crones to provide them. At the end of the fifth day of storytelling, Princess Zoza tells the tale of the false bride's deception, which brings about a sentence of death for the false bride. In a happy ending sequence, Prince Tadeo then marries Princess Zoza.

The overt sentiments Basile expressed in his tale collection were as distant from nobility as were his rank storytelling hags. The frame tale oozed crude social observations. "A seasoned proverb of ancient coinage says that those who look for what they should not, find what they would not."[7] In the next breath Basile produced a "ragged slave girl," whose duplicity would gain for her another's rightful husband, whose deceit would secure his affection, the last days of whose pregnancy would provide the occasion for telling the tales, and whose life ended in an ignominious execution.

Basile opened his frame tale not in a glorious and sacred church, like Boccaccio's Santa Maria Novella, but on a crowded and profane piazza. Low expletives and vulgar exposure replaced Boccaccio's elevated discourse. Boccaccio had taken his seven gracious and modest narrators from the rolls of Florentine nobility, but Basile turned to the Neapolitan rabble for his ten gossiping, razor-tongued, misshapen, diseased, and disorderly old bags whose coarse epithets matched their repellent appearances[8]: "lame Zeza, twisted Ceca, goitered Meneca, big-nosed Tolla, hunchback Popa, drooling Antonella, snout-faced Ciulla, cross-eyed Paola, mangy Ciommetella, and shitty Jacova."[9]

Both in Boccaccio's *Decameron* and in Basile's *Pentamerone*, the first order of the day was eating. Boccaccio's noble company had enjoyed a delicately prepared meal "in an orderly fashion," "joyously," and "with much merry talk" (1:25). They danced, sang, and the next day repaired to a pleasant meadow, a classic *locus amoenus*, where they might play chess before beginning to tell tales. In contrast, Basile's scruffy crowd, true to their base physicality, "slurp[ed] it up" before falling to their stories.[10] As for language, Basile's narrators put Neapolitan gutter talk into their characters' mouths.

There had been a long tradition of dialect literature in Naples, and by choosing dialect over elite usage, Basile was making a conscious literary and aesthetic choice. But he also laced his Neapolitan dialect with a comically elevated Baroque superfluity. Basile-as-author heaped up metaphors and piled on nouns, adjectives, and verbs. At the dawning of a new day "the Sun with the golden broom of his rays sweeps away the impurities of the Night from the fields sprinkled by the dawn." Sunset evokes the hour "when the sun, like a Genoese lady, draws the black taffeta round his face" while night "rises to light the candles of the catafalque of the heavens for the funeral obsequies of the Sun."[11] His linguistic oppositions of high and low style produced literary humor of the sort that would have provoked hearty laughter from a literarily sophisticated audience.

Into this literary mix, Basile inserted references from classical and medieval Christian texts, from medieval and Renaissance epics and popular print, and from contemporary life. His frame tale cited a pastoral drama well-known to his contemporaries,[12] while the comically ineffectual kings in his stories echoed Neapolitan street-theatre Pulcinellos. From the recent past he culled events that his listeners would have personally experienced.

Magic was an entirely different matter. In Basile's day, lively explorations of the marvelous and the occult occupied thinkers like Giordano Bruno and those around him in Naples and the South of Italy. In the literary arena, Giambattista Marino (1569–1625) had proclaimed that a poet must thirst for the marvelous and that whoever couldn't produce amazement in his readers and listeners should get work in a stable.[13] Amazement meant not only magical transformations and magically mediated endings, but also amazement brought about by the marvelous metaphors their creator used within the tale being told.[14] Basile followed this artistic ideal, and much of the plot material he introduced was drawn into a broad foundation by later European fairy tale authors, although his marvelous metaphors were quietly dropped.

Events that produced wonder and events that belonged to the world of the marvelous were not new in European entertainment. Baroque theater was filled with staged magic, flying chariots, and phantasmagoric lighting. In many churches statues of the crucified Christ bled anew in spring celebrations of the Passion and other statues made a real ascension through the church ceiling several weeks later. In preceding centuries, medieval sermon tales had been full of miracles that proved the blessedness of the lives of scores of saints. The effects of those medieval miracles' dramatic transformations and sudden salvations differed little from those produced by Baroque magic. But Basile's magic was not religiously based; it was thoroughly secular, in the sense that neither God nor a single saint was either invoked or credited with the remarkable transformations or sudden salvations that took place in his tales.

More prominent in Basile's tales is the kind of magic that suffused popular chivalric epics. And since magic, whether shape-shifting or otherworldly, had been absent from Boccaccio's tale collection, its presence in Basile's tales was yet another inversion of Boccaccio's exemplary work.[15]

LITERARY ACADEMIES AND BASILE

Literary academies, in their hundreds on the Italian peninsula, loomed large in the urban landscapes of the Renaissance and Baroque.[16] Not surprisingly, literary academies also loomed large in Basile's life. As a young man in his twenties on the island of Crete (then called Candia), he had joined the *Accademia degli Stravaganti*.[17] On his return to Naples he joined the *Accademia degli Oziosi* founded by the Spanish viceroy, the Count of Lemos, which also included the well-known poet Francisco de Quevedo.[18] Ten years later, in 1621, he became a member of the *Accademia degli Incauti*. It was in a cultural environment that included literary academies that Basile formulated what we now call his fairy tales, but there is currently no known evidence showing whether he first presented, or we might say "performed," his tales at academy meetings, in informal gatherings of friends and acquaintances, or as part of elegantly presented *conversazione* at any of the many small Neapolitan courts of his day.[19]

If Basile presented his tales to an audience, as there is every reason to believe he did, his audiences were noble, or like himself, ennobled, people with literary aspirations or literary pretensions. As Neapolitans, they lived as colonialized subjects of Spain, perhaps reluctantly, possibly willingly, or more likely in a complex combination of resentment and acceptance. They were above all courtiers, and they succeeded or suffered according to their ability to accommodate themselves to the visible and often irritating local presence of a Spanish overlord.

Basile's lifelong status as a courtier who was subject to the tastes of an overlord undoubtedly also played a role in his tale composition. In general, Basile's tales valorized noble protagonists and ridiculed foreign and poor ones.[20] The likelihood of a predominantly Neapolitan and noble audience for Basile's tales meant, first of all, that he and his audience may well have shared a preference for restoration tales with royal heroes and heroines who occupied center stage and who, if turned out from their palaces, were returned to wealth and power at the stories' conclusions.

Although the modern world prefers rise fairy tale plots, Basile's early modern collection has very few rise tales that magically reward a poor protagonist with marriage and wealth. Indeed, throughout Basile's collection the vulgar masses are rejected and depicted as repellent. Of the rise fairy tales that Straparola put into his collection, Basile used only "Costantino Fortunato" and "Pietro Pazzo" as models for rise fairy tales in the *Pentamerone*, "Cagliuso" (Day 2, Story 4) and "Peruonto" (Day 1, Story 3). Whether Basile took these two tales directly from Straparola's *Pleasant Nights* or whether they came to him through an intermediary we don't know.

Basile's "Cagliuso" recounts a "Puss in Boots" tale with a dying father and two sons, the younger of whom inherits the family cat. The cat catches fish and game and presents them to the king in the name of her master, whom she falsely titles Lord Cagliuso. She also devises strategies that get her master into the king's company dressed in rich clothing and make him an acceptable suitor for the king's lovestruck daughter. But despite the cat's role in Cagliuso's wedding to the princess and his consequent social rise to royal estate, at the end of the tale Cagliuso callously and ungratefully tosses her out the window, and she slinks away. Her fate, Basile adds, exemplifies the saying, "May God save you from the rich who become poor and from the beggar who has worked his way up."[21]

"Peruonto," Basile's version of Straparola's "Pietro Pazzo," has a yokel hero, whose appearance riding on a bunch of kindling makes little Princess Vastolla laugh. For this affront Peruonto revenges himself by wishing her pregnant with the magic he's gained by being kind to three fairies in the woods. Princess Vastolla eventually bears twin babies, and her father the king, having identified Peruonto as their father, angrily condemns them all to death by drowning in a barrel thrown into the sea. Peruonto, however, magically changes the barrel into a palace, they survive, he changes himself into a handsome fellow, and in the end everyone is happily reconciled.

"The Three Fairies" (Day 3, Story 10) and "The Two Little Pizzas" (Day 4, Story 7) are rise fairy tale variations on a single theme. In "The Three Fairies" a widow persecutes her beautiful and virtuous stepdaughter Cicella. But with the blessings of three fairies whom she helps, Cicella gains the love of a prince. Her stepmother succeeds in temporarily substituting her own unsightly daughter, Grannizia, but in the end inadvertently kills her with boiling water under the impression that she's getting rid of Cicella. Cicella and the prince marry. "The Two Little Pizzas" tells much the same story, except that the good and bad girls are not (step)sisters but two cousins, delightful Marziella with a "heart as beautiful as her face" and Puccia, with "the face of illness and the heart of plague."[22]

To his relatively rarely occurring painfully poor rise fairy tale protagonists, Basile added a few middle-class girls who gained a royal husband as well as a courtier who was rewarded with the hand of a princess. Viola (Day 2, Story 3), a respectable man's daughter, Sapia Liccarda (Day 3, Story 4) the daughter of a rich merchant, and the virtuous courtier Corvetto (Day 3, Story 7) all came from a social level safely above the beggary of Peruonto and Cagliuso. But in the words of their author these stories were not about the financial benefits of marrying up, but instead they exemplified a gender war won by a woman ("Viola"), the virtues of sexual moderation ("Sapia Liccarda"), and the punishment for harboring envy ("Corvetto"). Money figured neither in these tales' proverbs nor in their commentary. Neither did it do so in Straparola's "Ancilotto" (Night 4, Story 3), which similarly had a non-poor artisan's daughter who became a queen. Although in Straparola's tales money was positioned front and center and very positively when poor boys or girls married royally, Basile's rise fairy tale "Cagliuso" presented such a social rise as socially dangerous. In its concluding paragraph, the magic cat "ran off without once turning her head, [and] said, *May God save you from the rich who become poor and from the beggar who has worked his way up.*"[23]

Basile worked the long-traditional narrative trope of a girl-in-a-tower into the central element of his "Petrosinella" (Day 2, Story 1), the daughter of a "poor woman" (though it's not clear whether she's simply suffering or actually poverty-stricken). With the addition of extraordinarily long hair, he made its heroine the direct ancestor of generations of modern "Rapunzel" tales.

Let us return now to the issue of orality and fairy tales. Basile's texts, as we read them, are so well suited for performance that we must conclude that he composed at least some of them specifically for oral presentation. A virtual striptease at the end of his "Sole, Luna, e Talia" (Day 5, Story 5; Sun, Moon, and Talia) invites oral embroidery. We're in the palace courtyard. The husband of the titular heroine Talia has gone away, and in his absence his *other* wife—he's long been legally married to another woman—has just discovered that Talia has survived her—that is, the wife's—attempts to have her killed. Deeply irritated, the king's legitimate wife commands that a great fire be lit in the palace courtyard and that Talia be thrown into it. For her part, Talia sees "that things had taken a bad turn, [falls] down on her knees before the queen and [begs] her to at least give her the time to take off the clothes she [is] wearing."[24] Talia's wish to undress defies modern understanding, but within performance logic it functions perfectly, supplying cues for improvisational expressive commentary. And so the striptease continues as the Queen agrees, not out of pity, but because she wants to save the costly robes embroidered with gold and pearls for her own use.

Now the textual striptease begins. We may imagine listeners rapt with interest. Talia begins to undress, and with each garment she removes the text tells us that she utters a shriek. She takes off her dress [*the performer could here add "uuuuuuh"*], her skirt [*now an "ooooooh"*], her bodice [*"iiiiiiih"*], and is about to take off her petticoat [*"eeeeeeeeh" raising the tension*], and to utter her last cry [*"aaaaaaah"*]. Just when she is to be dragged away to be burned to ashes on a pyre, the King arrives, sees the spectacle, and rushes to her rescue. Basile's "Sun, Moon, and Talia" furnished Perrault with the plot and several of the characters for his "Sleeping Beauty," but the Parisian Perrault had left in place only a sly literary wink at his audience as a reminder of the Basile tale's raucous sexuality.

Basile incorporated many classical references into his tales, but they frequently occupied a higher plane. He took Diana and other characters from ancient literature and inserted them into his extravagant metaphors. He was surely on safe ground here, for every wellborn Neapolitan lad had studied precisely these figures in his Latin school texts. In the world of Basile's youth, classical figures were identified in Italian-language crib sheets; in the adult world they formed part of countless contemporary odes and were performed in operas. When Basile wanted to invoke sobriety, he eruditely referenced Heraclitus and Aristotle, sometimes to comic effect.

Basile's "Cinderella Cat" (Day 1, Story 6) offers the best possible definition of his style and content. Probably the world's most popular tale, the "Cinderella" known to the modern world made its first appearance in Basile's collection. (See chapter 3.) The *Pentamerone* summed up the tale this way:

> Zezolla, incited by her teacher to kill her stepmother, believes that she will be held dear for having helped the teacher to marry her father; instead she ends up in the kitchen. But due to the power of some fairies, after numerous adventures she wins a king for her husband.[25]

Modern-day readers have become accustomed to thinking of "Cinderella" tales as ones in which heroines rise from rags to riches, which is consistent with the ways in which the modern world privileges rise fairy tale plots. But as I've mentioned, Basile produced far more restoration plots than rise plots, and his "Cinderella Cat" is a case in point. Basile's Cinderella-heroine was not a poor girl who rose to riches, but a princess who was restored to the royal station from which first one and then another stepmother had displaced her. Even more interesting is the personality Basile created for her. Suffering from her first stepmother's mistreatment,

> the poor litle thing was always complaining to the teacher of her stepmother's ill treatment, saying "Oh, God, couldn't you be my little mommy, you who give me so many smooches and squeezes?" She repeated this so often that her teacher finally said, "If you follow the advice of this madcap, I'll become your mother and you'll be as dear to me as the pupils of these eyes." Zezolla interrupted her and said, "Forgive me if I take the words out of your mouth. I know you love me dearly, so mum's the word, and *sufficit*; teach me the trade, for I'm new in town; you write and I'll sign." Her teacher answered, "[L]isten carefully; keep your ears open and your bread will come out as white as flowers. As soon as your father leaves, tell your stepmother you want one of those old dresses in the big chest in the storeroom so that you can save the one you're wearing. Since she likes to see you all patched up in rags, she'll open the chest and say, 'Hold the lid up.' And as you're holding it while she rummages around inside, let it bang shut, and she'll break her neck."[26]

A discreet elision of the dreadful deed leads directly to the post-mortem grieving that followed her first step-mother's death: "once the mourning for her stepmother's accident was over [. . .]"[27]In Basile's tale the new wife has not two, but six greedy daughters who torment the suffering heroine. Help, however, comes from a dove of the fairies who sends Cinderella a potted date tree along with elegant tools to care for it. The tree grows wondrously, and when her stepsisters try to prevent her from

going to a festival that the king will be attending, the date tree
outfits her like a queen. No one knows who the beautiful visitor
is, and when she departs from the palace at the end of the fes-
tivities, royal servants chase after her, trying to learn her identity. In her haste, she loses a shoe. The king gazes upon her
patten, a wooden shoe of the kind meant to raise a lady's foot
and her fine gown above the gummy mud of city streets; he
rhapsodizes about the Neapolitan equivalent of serviceable
galoshes and imagines the foot it had held, the leg it had supported, and about what lies beyond:

> If the foundations (*the prince speaks here of the patten*) are
> so beautiful, what must be the house be like? O lovely
> candlestick that held the candle that consumes me! O
> tripod of the charming cauldron in which my life is boil-
> ing! O beautiful corks, attached to the fishing line of
> Love used to catch this soul! There: I'll embrace and
> squeeze you; if I cannot reach the plant, I will adore its
> roots, and if I cannot have the capitals, I will kiss its
> base! You were once the memorial stone for a white foot,
> and now you are a snare for this black heart. You made
> the lady who tyrannizes this life a span and a half taller,
> and you make this life grow just as much in sweetness, as
> I contemplate and possess you.[28]

Basile's wildly Baroque style limited the lifespan of his work;
his simple story plots, however, made admirable literary tem-
plates and transplanted easily. Hence the fairy tales that sprang
from his quirky collection—"Sun, Moon, and Talia," "The Cinderella Cat," "The Seven Little Pork Rinds," "Nennillo and
Nennella," "Petrosinella," "The Bear"—were tamed, that is,
edited, and in their subdued form slipped seamlessly into a
broadly accepted, and acceptable, tradition as "Sleeping Beauty,"
"Cinderella," "Rumpelstiltskin," "Hansel and Gretel," "Rapunzel," and "Donkeyskin." Basile's "Peruonto" spread throughout

the world in forms close to the version he'd written, but because
of the story's vulgarity, Perrault rejected it and the Grimms
changed it nearly beyond recognition. It therefore remains relatively unknown among western fairy tale readers.[29]

Of the Basile stories listed here, only a few have literary
antecedents in terms of their plots, but his "Sun, Moon, and
Talia" (Basile's "Sleeping Beauty" tale) has a long literary line-
age. It derives from an Italian translation of a late medieval
French romance, *Perceforest*, itself based on Spanish and Cat-
alonian precursors. But that Basilean tale-with-a-history is an
exception, because the great majority of the tales in the modern
fairy tale canon that took their first shape with Basile often did
so by amalgamating preexisting motifs, not by springing from
preexisting *plots* in the way that "Sun, Moon, and Talia" did.

Basile's fairy tales have plots that seem to have been conceived primarily as vehicles for his subverting humor and his listeners' complicit enjoyment. That is, the tales whose plots occur
first in Basile's *Pentamerone* seem to be a kind of literary accident
incidental to their performance aspect.

Basile's writing, admired in his own day, fell from favor when
later generations saw his bombastic Baroque poetics as old-fash-
ioned. But his constructive narrative talent was so great that his
stories—stripped of their schoolboy lewdness and timebound
rhetoric—provided enduringly engaging plots that later writers
were able to adopt and adapt for their own purposes. That is precisely what happened in late seventeenth-century Paris, when
first Perrault together with his niece Mlle Lhéritier used his plots
to produce tales that courteous and well-mannered late seventeenth-century *salonistes* would find both diverting and acceptable. (See chapter 3.)

Fairy tale scholars have often asked themselves if Basile
knew Straparola's Venetian tales. It would be surprising if he had
not known them. After all, Basile had lived in Venice in the
early 1600s, at a time when Straparola's collection was still in
print and being sold there, and so his tales would have been

within easy reach. In Naples, Basile and his acquaintances might also have known Straparola's collection, since Venetian books were distributed throughout the Italian peninsula, and Naples itself was a major consumer of Venetian print. But Straparola's tales differed from Basile's in many respects, and so it makes sense now to turn to the coinventor of European fairy tales, Giovan Francesco Straparola, whose works permeate the literary layer beneath Basile.

GIOVAN FRANCESCO STRAPAROLA: *LE PIACEVOLI NOTTI*

It was Giovan Francesco Straparola who created rise fairy tales, and he did so at the end of his life, when he was in his late sixties or early seventies. In the five decades between his arrival in Venice in the early 1500s and his return to the publishing scene in 1551, he had probably survived by ghostwriting for one of Venice's busy *salonistes* whose daytime labors left little time to burnish bright witticisms or to compose elegant madrigals. Many writers survived in Renaissance Venice on the pay they earned as professional translators, editors, and ghostwriters. Straparola's own writing makes it clear that he knew Venice and had experienced the repelling reek of rank poverty and had known the beguiling softness of great wealth.

Straparola compiled a book of stories called *Le Piacevoli Notti* (Pleasant Nights). He structured it in imitation of Boccaccio's *Decameron*, with an external event bringing together a group of men and women. In *The Pleasant Nights* it was Ottaviano Maria Sforza's sudden and fiction-embellished loss of political power in Milan that was made to account for his removal to the island of Murano together with his daughter and a group of friends.[30] (An earlier tale compiler, Giovanni Sercambi, had also chosen that island, which lies just a few hundred meters off the northern Venetian *riva*, for a storytelling assembly.) Straparola had thirteen nights instead of Boccaccio's ten, and on each night he had only five, or sometimes six, stories until the thirteenth, when there were thirteen. Most of Straparola's stories can be traced to known precursors, with the thirteen stories of the thirteenth night coming mostly from Girolamo Morlini's Latin-language *Novellae* (1520).

Straparola was literarily conservative, or conservationist, having also turned to medieval romances and epics, as well as to Ariosto's more recent extensions of the Orlando cycle. From these sources he had cobbled together several fairy tales about princes and princesses who—having fallen or having been pushed from their royal positions—embarked on adventures that eventually returned them to a palace. Heroines like Doralice (Night 1, Story 4) had a very hard time of it before escaping near death.[31] In another tale Biancabella's hands were cut off because of a wicked stepmother (Night 3, Story 3), but magic enabled her to produce instant and imposing architecture as part of a strategy to win back her husband and restore herself to her palace. It was thoroughly characteristic of restoration fairy tales that their heroes and heroines, like Biancabella, used magic actively to bring about their returns to royal ranks. Restoration fairy tale heroes like Livoretto (Night 3, Story 2) and Guerrino (Night 5, Story 1) went out into the world with powerful magic helpers whose special gifts they cannily used.[32] It's worth noting in passing that heroes' and heroines' antagonists in Straparola's fairy tales aren't always evil, as they are in modern ones. In Livoretto's tale, the Sultan of Cairo was simply older and less handsome than his wife fancied.

Among the restoration fairy tales Straparola had put together from popular romances, he inserted a handful of newly created stories, rise fairy tales. Most of them depicted the afflictions of poverty in graphic terms. One heroine had to share her marital bed with a pig[33]; another hero suffered from scurvy and was covered with mange until his cat licked him clean.[34] Others endured beatings from their masters.[35]

The miserable condition of Venice's poor as depicted in Straparola's *Pleasant Nights* is confirmed in socio-historical studies like Brian Pullan's *Rich and Poor in Renaissance Venice* and "Town Poor, Country Poor." Guido Ruggiero's sidelights on living conditions in *Boundaries of Eros* also illuminate living conditions in sixteenth-century Venice, and so do Robert C. Davis's accounts of poor people's diversions in *War of the Fists*. What modern historians teach us is the same thing that literate artisans living within a contracting mid-century Venetian economy knew for themselves: for the most part, dreams of improving their lot could only be a dream, a hope, or a wish.

In the late 1540s and early 1550s Straparola developed the new plot in which poor folks left poverty behind, not by working hard, not by seducing a wealthy boy, girl, man, or woman, and then marrying up the social scale, and certainly not by marrying a member of the remote and inaccessible Venetian nobility. The marriage of members of the nobility outside their legally-defined group had been effectively, and legally, forbidden since the 1520s. On the contrary Straparola's stories proposed that a poor boy or girl could, with magical intervention, marry a prince or a princess in a faraway land and become rich.

In real life Renaissance Venice, magic was as elusive as class-vaulting marriages. Neither did Venice have princes and princesses. What Venice *did* have was a small population of noble and visibly wealthy families who lived among a large population of poor people, most of whom could read and were therefore potential consumers of escapist narratives of magically mediated upward mobility through a marriage that brought wealth to its poor protagonist.

Judged by its popularity over the long term, Straparola's most successful literary creation was the first tale of the eleventh night now known as "Puss in Boots." If Straparola had given it a title, it would have been "Costantino Fortunato," because that was the name of its poor hero whose fate was reshaped by a fairy in the shape of a gray brindle cat. Straparola's barepawed puss trapped small game and carried it to a king whose good will she further fostered with skillful flattery. She made her dirt-poor master look good by licking the mange from his filthy skin, bathing him, and, by a foresighted stratagem, having him clothed by the king himself in royal robes. And finally, she used canny trickery to win the king's approval for his daughter's marriage to the penniless Costantino. It ended well, when further trickery, augmented by a large dollop of good luck, landed Costantino in a castle of his own.

Straparola's tale made a brief appearance in Basile's collection, lived on in Perrault's barely reworked version, and exploded into popularity in nineteenth-century England, France, Germany, and America. Straparola's other rise and restoration tales survived in reworkings by late seventeenth-century French authors, through whom they passed whole or in part into the German storytelling tradition.

Among Straparola's rise fairy tale heroines there is the lovely but impoverished Meldina in Night 2, Story 1 mentioned above, who accepted for her husband a casually murderous pig who loved rolling in the muck before he came to bed.[36] There is also Adamantina in Night 5, Story 2 with barely a crust in her house until a magic doll enters her life, defecates gold, and gets her married to a king.[37] Straparola's heroes of rise fairy tales include the fool Pietro (poor, stupid, ugly, and vicious until significantly improved in looks, intelligence, and manners by his princess) and Dionigi (Night 8, Story 4), languid in learning a trade but adept at acquiring magic (although he suffered many a beating before he, too, got a royal bride through magic).[38] Magic made Costantino (Night 11, Story 1) handsome when his fairy cat licked him clean. Other characters in rise fairy tales simply went directly from their impoverished state to a royal chamber. This accelerated social rise hints that Straparola directed his rise fairy tales toward poor readers who were like the heroes and heroines of these stories and could identify with them and could have hoped to share their good fortune. But from the richly bound surviving copies of Straparola's books we can also infer a wealthy or well-to-do readership that could easily have laughed heartily at the absurdity of rise fairy tale plots without identifying with their down-and-out heroes and heroines.

Straparola practiced and produced several imperfect rise fairy tales before he created "Costantino Fortunato." The world's first perfected rise fairy tale, it represents the apogee of his literary achievement, and therefore merits close attention. It begins with three brothers and their dying mother. She has little enough to bequeath: the two older, mean-spirited boys get a kneading trough and a pastry board, the youngest, a cat. The cat, however, was none other than a fairy in disguise, who immediately set out to improve Costantino's unlucky lot. First she ingratiated herself with the king with gifts of wild game that she cleverly caught, then she engineered a meeting between him and Costantino. Cleaned up and in royal garments, Costantino captured his daughter's heart; the king dowered her richly; and they married soon after. The cat for her part cleverly secured a castle for the newlyweds. "Not long after this," so Straparola ended his story, the princess's father "died, and by acclamation the people chose Costantino as their king, seeing that he had married Elisetta, the late king's daughter, to whom the kingdom belonged by right of succession. And by these means Costantino rose from poverty or even beggary to become a powerful king, and he lived a long time with Elisetta, his wife, leaving their children to inherit his kingdom."

Straparola's story bears some resemblance to England's Dick Whittington in that it circles around a poor boy, a cat, and the acquisition of great wealth. But Dick Whittington, who shipped abroad with his cat and rid a sultan's kingdom of mice (or rats, depending on the version), received his wealth in return for a job well done. When he returned home rich, he married and eventually became Lord Mayor of London. Each story, "Dick Whittington" and "Costantino Fortunato," has a poor hero and a cat who mediates wealth. Each hero marries and ascends to a powerful position. On the other hand, there is no magic *per se* in the English "Dick Whittington," since his cat simply did what cats do, namely chase, catch, and eat mice (or rats), although admittedly in great numbers. In "Costantino," it is a magically speaking cat who directs events and an ogre's magical shape-shifting that provides a castle. But the real differences lie in the order in which things happen. Dick Whittington realistically achieves wealth *before* he marries, a sequence that is consistent with medieval and early modern social practice. Straparola's "Costantino," however, has an impoverished hero who gets his wealth by magically marrying a princess, which is not at all consistent with standard social practice in the Renaissance.

The defining sequence in Straparola's rise fairy tales is this:

poverty → magic → marriage → wealth.

This sequence represents that rarity in narrative history, a wholly new plotline. It was Straparola's invention, and it was his great contribution to the European literary tradition.

Straparola made many textual mistakes in the frame tale and in his stories that escaped correction before the book was published: trees leaf out in January, a character is called by the wrong name, information is occasionally repeated, or worse, is omitted. Editorial haste, everywhere evident, suggests that no copy editor tidied up his manuscript before taking it to the printshop. But Straparola's achievement in having created a revolutionary plot line far outweighs the drawbacks of the book's occasionally sloppy style.

A thorough search through magic encounters in Boiardo's and Ariosto's earlier *Orlando* epics produces nothing like Straparola's rise fairy tales. Neither does a close examination of fifteenth- and sixteenth-century Italian popular print. The only relevant tale that predates Straparola's rise fairy tales is a 1470 Venice edition of a story entitled *Lionbruno*.

LIONBRUNO: A POPULAR ROMANCE,
BUT NOT (YET) A FAIRY TALE

Lionbruno features a boy who marries up, includes numerous elements typical of fairy tales (such as the number three); a youngest son; a transformation of a beautiful damsel (into a bird); a lengthy journey accomplished in seconds; tasks and trials; and a wedding that unites the story's poor boy to a girl in a castle.

This sounds like a fairy tale. Indeed, the plot as summarized sounds just like a rise fairy tale, but significant differences separate the ones that Straparola created eighty years later from the 1470 story of *Lionbruno*: In return for a rich catch of fish and lots of gold and silver an impoverished father delivers his seven-year-old son, Lionbruno, to the Devil. However, the boy saves himself from the Devil's power by making the sign of the cross. Shortly thereafter an eagle carries Lionbruno swiftly to a distant castle, and then turns into a ten-year-old virgin named Madonna Aquilina. She remains a virgin for the next eight years, during which time she provides Lionbruno "with a master who taught him well, and he learned to use a sword and to joust. In the use of arms he became a famous champion, and no one could stand up against his blows, so that everyone in that country said, 'This must be the son of a count or a baron, so gallant is he and so handsome in appearance.'"

When he has grown up, Madonna Aquilina asks Lionbruno, now an accomplished (and therefore acceptable) suitor, to marry her. He agrees, and they become man and wife. In this story it was not magic that made the poor Lionbruno acceptable in the eyes of the royal Madonna Aquilina, but courtly accomplishments achieved by eight years of careful study and practice. *Lionbruno* also differs from classic rise fairy tales as they existed from Straparola onward in the narrative placement of the hero or heroine's wedding. In rise fairy tales a wedding characteristically marks a story's culmination, but in *Lionbruno* the hero's wedding occurs one quarter of the way through the tale, after which the bulk of the tale's adventures take place.

Lionbruno's adventures utilize motifs that would later become the stock in trade of both rise and restoration fairy tales: enchanted doors; a magic ring that grants wishes; a time-limited journey home; a prohibition (here, that the hero not speak his wife's name to others); an instantaneous passage to a distant destination; a crossing over into an alien culture (Saracen Granada); seven-league boots; and a cloak of invisibility.

At the Granada court, Lionbruno enters the lists against a Saracen warrior. When the Saracen king consults his barons about Lionbruno, the barons air some very unfairytale-like suspicions. "What do you know of this person?" they ask with worldly wisdom. They object that "[h]e does not seem to be of such noble condition as would make him our equal, although he is brave and full of prowess. . . ."

Rise fairy tales never base objections to an aspiring hero on such realistic grounds. Furthermore, objections in a fairy tale are typically set by a figure who embodies raw wickedness, figures such as a false and jealous wife, a hateful mother-in-law, a spiteful stepmother, or a cannibal queen. Fairy tale impediments ignore or bypass real social objections against marriage across class boundaries by projecting them onto outlandish characters. But in 1470 the world of Straparola's rise fairy tale did not yet exist. Hence the barons and the barons' plan to find the truth about the unknown warrior. "Let everyone boast of something that they can be required to show evidence of actually existing," they say. And through this device Lionbruno is brought to boast of Madonna Aquilina, whom he must produce on pain of losing his head. Since she had forbidden him to speak of her, his boast breaks the bond that had joined them, and Lionbruno loses not only his wife but also the favor he had won by his valor in the Granada tournament.

The first part of the *Lionbruno* narrative ended with magic withdrawn from its hero and with his falling among a band of

robbers. The printed text incorporates textual markers for perfor-
mative presentation, and at this point it closes for a break—for
lunch, for drinks, or perhaps for gathering coins from the listeners, or if individuals had to go on their way, for selling them a
copy of the printed *Lionbruno* text to reread later.

Lionbruno as it has survived into the modern world is a
printed text that contains within it evidence of public oral performance. Its close linkage of the privately written to the publicly spoken word has many parallels in the early modern period.
Two sixteenth-century books, Baldassare Castiglione's *Book of the
Courtier* (1528) and Girolamo Bargagli's *Dialogue on Games*
(written 1563, first published 1572) both make specific recom-
mendations about how to tell a story and what stories to tell
(preferably ones from Boccaccio's *Decameron*) when called upon
to provide entertainment at court or among academy members
and their guests. Nor was the public storytelling of written works
solely a pastime of the privileged. Rudolf Schenda reports evidence for the "primary importance for the oral diffusion of
printed material" in a number of European locations among the
semi-literate.[39]

In the second part of *Lionbruno* we learn that the robbers
Lionbruno has just joined have murdered two merchants, stolen
their money, and helped themselves to two magic objects, a
cloak of invisibility and a pair of seven-league boots. The robbers, quarreling over the division of their booty, ask Lionbruno
to mediate. He tries on the cloak and boots and, now invisible,
speeds on his way, escaping with the stolen money.

Lionbruno's quest for the lost Madonna Aquilina follows. It
is fraught with impossible tasks that he accomplishes with help
from Jesus, the Virgin Mary, an old hermit, an angel from
heaven, the Southeast Wind, and, of course, the seven-league
boots. When Lionbruno finally re-finds Madonna Aquilina's
castle, he approaches her unseen, under the cloak of invisibility.
To remind her of himself, he kisses her. Still unseen, he hears her
lament their separation. Ultimately she catches him out and

"they threw their arms about each other with the truest love, and upon that bed they made their peace."

The scene of connubial bliss in which Lionbruno and Madonna Aquilina make their peace with one another on a nuptial bed ends *Lionbruno*. This narrative is not a fairy tale, but a medieval romance. Stripped to its bare bones, it could be presented in a relatively brief span of time to an audience that was in all likelihood composed principally of urban listeners taking their ease during a break from work.

Lionbruno, not a fairy tale, was also not a rise fairy tale. Neither was the ninth-century tale in which it was predicted that King Solomon's daughter would marry a penniless boy.[40] The union took place as foreseen, but what the marriage between social unequals showed was not that a poor boy could marry a princess, but that through God nothing is impossible.[41]

Dig where we may, no rise fairy tales can be found in layers of literary remains before Straparola. Not a single one exists contemporary with or before *Lionbruno* or contemporary with the handful of rise and restoration fairy tales in Straparola's *Pleasant Nights*.

As far as *restoration* fairy tales are concerned, lengthy romances abound in that era, and some of them would later be turned into restoration fairy tales. Before Straparola, however, only one such tale existed in a sufficiently brief form to be considered kin to Straparola's restoration fairy tales. It was called *Asinarius* and was a purpose-built abbreviation of a longer romance for a Latin schoolbook, its brevity a schoolroom artifact.[42]

Brief magical tales also survive from medieval sermon tale collections. With an omnipresent magically miraculous salvational Christianity, they often incorporate motifs that would later become familiar through their reappearance in early modern fairy tales. Medieval preachers told tales that reinforced religious belief, but one searches in vain among Europe's thousands of sermon tales for a single rise fairy tale.

Fairy tale motifs abound in the late medieval period, as is evident from Lionbruno's cloak of invisibility and his seven-league boots. The same is true of another (inversion of a) modern motif, the wild woman who had to be kissed in Giulia Bigolina's novel *Urania*. But despite the existence of one fairy tale motif after another, not a single rise fairy tale was composed until Giovan Francesco Straparola produced Europe's first ones. This simple perception has been either discounted or disputed by generations of fairy tale scholars, as the final chapter will show.

FIVE

A NEW HISTORY

If we look forward from Straparola toward the fairy tale future, we see a publishing phenomenon with printed texts carrying fairy tales from one place to another. The ubiquitous and mysterious folk and nursemaids remain, but as consumers of fairy tales rather than as producers.

The publishing history of fairy tales shows that these stories were associated first with the literate classes and secondarily with the less-lettered folk. Madame d'Aulnoy's *Les contes des fées* (The Tales of the Fairies, 1697) began as four-volume productions whose internal reference points were unidirectionally upper-class, but within a single generation the *bibliothèque bleue* was providing cheap imprints of individual d'Aulnoy stories for a market of simpler and generally poorer readers. The same process was repeated in greater detail and with more textual changes in Britain. There Mme d'Aulnoy's tales, translated into English, were twice printed for upper class readers, a readership unmistakeably addressed in their prefaces. A reworked translation directed at merchants' wives, with amendments appropriate for that less exalted readership, came out with a variety of publishers in the next twenty years, while a third bowdlerized and simplified translation, was meant for humble readers. (Only after fairy tales had proven their success in the chapbook trade did the enterprising London publisher Mary Cooper and the renowned publisher of books for children John Newbery take them up for young readers.[1])

What then of the role of the folk in the creation of fairy tales? Although there have been many assertions and assumptions about the unlettered populus producing fairy tales in the early modern period, documentary evidence shows the opposite, with *listening* rustics being the recipients of stories read aloud to them by the literate. Rudolf Schenda, demonstrating this repeatedly in his study of European narrative, *Von Mund zu Ohr* (From Mouth to Ear, 1993), cited countless instances in which the German Enlightenment educator of the masses, Rudolph Zacharias Becker, read aloud in towns and villages.[2] Distinguishing among several kinds of non-literate acquisition of knowledge of printed stories, Schenda called the practice of reading to people who couldn't themselves read a *semi-literate* process and a teller's repeating previously read material to others a *semi-oral* process.[3] In both processes books played a manifestly central role.

In the early history of the Grimms' collecting, books for the middle and upper classes are once again implicated. The Grimms' most prolific fairy tale informants (just a reminder once again that I'm discussing fairy tales and not folk tales; see chapter 1 for the distinctions underlying this discussion) were middle- and upper-middle class bookreaders. In the 1830s, after the Grimms had published their First, Second, and Third Large Editions, as well as their First, Second, and Third Small Editions of the *Nursery and Household Tales*, selected tales from their collection were introduced into German elementary school readers. Ingrid Tomkowiak has shown how those tales influenced generations of German children, who often memorized them as standard classroom practice.[4] By the twentieth century the Grimms' tales had become an unquestioned component of German childhood.[5] Formal and wide-ranging studies of colonial schooling and of the textbooks used in colonial schools have not yet been carried out, but informal conversations suggest that schoolbooks

used in schools set up by European colonial governments disseminated national fairy tale canons into Africa, Asia, and the
Caribbean in much the same manner in which chapbooks had
earlier carried French fairy tales into French Canada and into
pockets of French population along the Mississippi.[6]

THE CONSEQUENCES OF A BOOK-BASED
HISTORY OF FAIRY TALES

A history of fairy tales based on named authors and book transmission has thoroughgoing consequences. The first is political,
and was central to the rhetoric of the Grimms' nineteenth-century political agenda. It was an intellectual agenda with real-
world consequences, since large parts of it were adopted by the
very Prussian government that supported the Grimms from
1840 onwards. The Grimms held that language determined
nationality, a view that ratified the political incorporation of
the then-Danish-governed Schleswig-Holstein into German-
speaking Prussia, because the inhabitants of Schleswig-Holstein
spoke a language that Jacob Grimm judged to be far more
German than Danish.

The second area on which revising a belief in folk origins of
fairy tales has an impact is related, but slightly different. The
Grimms believed an individual's knowledge of brief narratives
(Märchen) proved the existence of a common national folk heritage that had generated those narratives. That is, Jacob and
Wilhelm assumed that a single person's knowledge of a tale stood
for a shared knowledge of that tale by the entire population from
which that person came. The Grimms didn't test this assumption, nor was it scrutinized by later scholars, but it was nonetheless embraced by folklorists internationally. It would have been
easy for the Grimms to ascertain a relationship between a
person's having read a story in a book and that person's remem-
bering it and later recounting it to them; they would only have

had to ask their informant a few questions about their current and earlier reading habits. But since both Grimms were unshakeably convinced that the tales they heard resulted from a centuries-long chain of unbroken oral transmission from the ancient past, they never thought to ask their informants about where— either in general or in particular—they had learned the stories they told the brothers.

A book-based history of fairy tales explains the remarkable phenomenon of similar or identical tellings of the same story by different storytellers. Similarities in wording and phrasing in a particular story has frequently been observed by European and American collectors of fairy tales in the field, even when the same story is told by two or three different individuals. This observation led past folklorists to think about the powers of folk memory, and most concluded that such similarities demonstrated that folk memory was unvarying and perfect. Indeed, the Grimms themselves concluded that it was the simplicity of simple people's lives that made it possible for them to retain a story without changing it. Folk memory was invoked most famously when late nineteenth-century French tellings of "Red Riding Hood" agreed in every detail with Charles Perrault's text from nearly two hundred years before. And yet book history, and the presence of specific texts in particular places at particular times (as, for example, in schools where children memorized it or in towns whose local newspaper published it or in homes where a popular book might exist at several addresses) offer an equally good, and in many respects, a better explanation for similar or identical tellings of a single story. Intranational narrative mutualities such as schools, newspapers, and books were far more likely to have been responsible for the extent to which a body of fairy tales was disseminated within any given society, whether that society was Danish, Norwegian, Swedish, Finnish or Russian, or any of those of southern and southeastern Europe. International plot similarities can be accounted for by book transmission far more logically than they can be by oral transmission. Many of the plots of French fairy tales were born south of the Alps in Venice and in the shadow of Vesuvius in Naples.

In a large sense the international spread of fairy tales can be explained within a history of a predominantly Italian creation, French editing, and German re-editing that took place in a context of commercial mechanisms within book distribution networks. Fairy tales can be shown to have arrived in a new location and to have been documented there in concert with the arrival of the books bearing those fairy tales. The most dramatic incidence is perhaps the highly likely arrival of Basilean fairy tales in France in the hands of their printer and publisher Antonio / Antoine Bulifon in the late 1680s or early 1690s, directly after which Charles Perrault, Mlle Lhéritier, and others began (re)create many of the same tales.

A book-based history of fairy tales cracks the foundations on which many psychologists have created purpose-built interpretations of fairy tales. Without the broad and anonymous folk as the ultimate author of fairy tales, Bruno Bettelheim's notion that fairy tales represent essential aspects of the human psyche must be revised. Perhaps fairy tales are better understood not as a direct and unmediated expression of human beings' emotional need, but as people's conscious or unconscious incorporation of tales that suit their needs which canny suppliers recognize and respond to.[7] A close, even intimate, connection remains between fairy tales and the public, so that the end result remains—the extraordinary popularity of certain fairy tales. But the mechanisms by which a widespread popularity is understood to have come about differ considerably in a book-based explication.

Fairy tales' marketability is a key element in their history. Measurable by the extent to which the public consumed them, marketability is an indirect rather than a direct[8] form of evidence for human longings and individual hopes as expressed in specific fairy tales. But printings and reprintings of fairy tales as a measure of public acceptance, and even more than that, of public consumption of fairy tales, *is* evidence in an area of study where evidence has for a long time been very scarce indeed.[9]

We still remain ignorant of many things about fairy tales in the history of book printing and publishing. For instance, we don't know the precise number of copies that each print run produced in past centuries, although for books for the general market, 1,000 copies per print run is generally taken as a norm. On the other hand, *re*printings reveal a great deal about the public's preferences. People buy books that speak to their condition, that appeal to them in one way or another, that their friends, acquaintances, and relatives recommend to them, and above all, people buy books that they like. Fairy tale books were bought in increasing numbers in the eighteenth and nineteenth centuries. As fairy tales were marketed to an increasingly broad public, rise fairy tales represented a growing proportion of tale content in books of fairy tales. As a whole, the predominance of rise over restoration fairy tales gained steadily in the nineteenth-, twentieth-, and twenty-first centuries.

Each observation about hard fairy tale data—the number of fairy tale books printed, the number of print runs a particular fairy tale book had, the number of translations a single story had, the number of books in a print run—opens a window onto the book-buying public's taste for fairy tales, and each one makes that taste measurable in countable numbers of book sales. Many more case studies are needed, but the direction is apparent and well documented in a study like "The Relationship between Oral and Literary Tradition as a Challenge in Finnish Fairy-Tale Research" by the Finnish scholar Satu Apo. Increasingly, the study of cheap print, such as pocket books and newspapers, shows written sources spreading a broad knowledge of what has long been considered traditional oral material. So far this has been documented in nineteenth- and early twentieth-century Finland, Brittany, Ireland, and England,[10] and additional research are likely to confirm these initial findings.

Folklorists' observations in the nineteenth and twentieth centuries were for the most part accurate accounts of tales that their informants knew and told them (although there is a large and growing body of scholarship devoted to the way in which past folklorists edited the materials they collected, sometimes changing them fundamentally). How today's folklorists understand the past record, however, depends on their theoretical stance.

Growing amounts of evidence indicate that known authors created fairy tales and that printing and publishing practices were central to their dissemination. The evidence requires an adjustment to continuing insistence that fairy tales originated among an unlettered folk and that fairy tales in books contaminated pure folk productions. Similarly, fairy tales' plot and language stability underlies an unquestioned assumption that tales' transmission has depended on oral means. This assumption suffuses the laws and theories of folk narrative and has created a major impediment to understanding fairy tales' history over long stretches of time and even longer geographical distances.

It is an observable fact that over time some tales have changed in their style, content, and structure, an observation at odds with the assumption that fairy tales have remained stable and invariant over the long term. These two competing observations have produced a central paradox in the theory and history of folk narrative, one that has never been logically accounted for. That is, how can the folk be producers and perfect rememberers at the same time that they are variers and alterers?

The Grimms were the initial providers of reasons to account for the perfection they claimed for folk memory, although their reasons made little sense, were offensively condescending, and remain experimentally unsupported. Theories have been developed in abundance to explain the paradox of evident stability in content along with content and stylistic change. One is that oral micro-conduits provide competing and alternative modes of narrative transport. But this kind of theory is unnecessary when content is maintained in a translated book or when style is changed in order to sell books to a new market. Bookselling practices explain content continuity and stylistic change far more effectively than does a theory of oral micro-conduits. Micro-conduits themselves, as Linda Dégh and A. Vázsonyi conceptualized them, accurately account for the circulation of differing print versions of a single story in a given culture. In fact, in most cases, existing folk narrative "laws" remain tenable if book routes are substituted for the oral ones that they posit.[11]

The true scandal of the oralist-privileging history of traditional fairy tale studies has been the suppression of evidence about the status of individual storytellers. Imagine a blind storyteller who was presented as a perfect example of a completely oral transmitter of story tradition, who—because of his blindness—remained utterly uncontaminated by book-based story sources. Such is the "history" of one "oral" source, and consensual belief among folklorists produced more than one completely uncontaminated storyteller. The outrageous instance outlined above involved a blind storyteller in Finland who was known as "Blind Strömberg." Blind Strömberg's blindness made him a posterboy for the theory that fairy tales had been transmitted orally: his blindness both denoted and connoted an inability to have *read* the tales he told as an adult. But the facts of Blind Strömberg's life were inconveniently different. Young Strömberg had been a sighted child and an avid reader who became blind at the age of ten. The shocking part of the history of Blind Strömberg is that those who first chronicled his storytelling knew of his earlier reading and of his later blindness and conscientously included those facts in their accounts. But researchers eager to demonstrate the existence of oral transmission erased all mention of Blind Strömberg's childhood reading. This remarkable history was laid out by the Finnish researcher Gun Herranen in a cautionary 1989 article, "A Big Ugly Man with a Quest for Narratives," which deserves close reading.

As far as definitions are concerned, a rigorous separation of tales about fairies and fairy tales from folk tales has perhaps a greater consequence, because it requires an active recognition of differences in their plots, characters, construction, performance, and above all, in the history of the three genres.

THEORIES OF FAIRY TALE ORIGINS

The most influential theory of the origins and spread of folk and fairy tales was developed in the later nineteenth century. Called the geographic-historical method, it was enunciated and developed by Julius Krohn (1835–1888) and further elaborated by his son Kaarle Krohn (1863–1933). Demanding in detail and scholarly in outlook, the geographic-historical method resulted in a host of enormously useful reference works. But the geographic-historical method depended on the concept of oral transmission, and it gave birth to an oralist-privileging vocabulary which declares to this day that printed tales represent a "contamination" of "pure" orality.

Believing that oral transmission preceded and underlay all tales that had been told, including fairy tales, it follows naturally that an illiterate, non-literate, preliterate, or aliterate population was necessarily responsible for fairy tales' composition. That logical necessity produced the idea that folk-authoring and the tales authored by the folk grew from, and therefore incorporated, folk experience. Arnold van Gennep (1873–1957) described tales as verbal representations of cultural rites of passage: Rapunzel in her tower, for example, was for him an instance of sequestration at menarche. Is there a problem with van Gennep's reasoning? Sequestering a girl when her menstrual period begins was a practice observed by twentieth-century anthropologists in some exotic cultures, but "Rapunzel" is a European tale. Neither the towered girls in Ovid's *Metamorphoses* nor ones in the Neapolitan society within which Rapunzel's tale first appeared practiced tower sequestration at menarche. Nonetheless, since van Gennep came up with his theory, anything red has frequently been interpreted as a narrative ritually associated with female sexual maturation. Red Riding Hood's cloak figures large in these discussions, but so do red apples and red cheeks.

Most of the conclusions reached by nineteenth- and twentieth-century oralist folklorists were based on phenomena they had observed in the field. They found people telling the same or similar tales in locations far distant from one another. That is a fact, and it is clear enough. But because they viewed their evidence through a lens skewed by nationalistic and folkloristic agendas they came to distorted conclusions. There was no room in their theories for fairy tales' historical origins among urban authors, with reproduction via printing presses and dissemination along bookselling routes.

Folklore began as the study of the lore of the folk, hence the name the discipline took for itself. Folklore studies today encompass very different subjects, such as foodways, the use of space, and media relationships. As a result, the study of fairy and folk tales occupies a relatively small corner of folklore studies, and the tangled issue of fairy tales' origins and dissemination an even smaller space. Because fairy tales no longer lie at the center of folklore studies, views about fairy tales' origins and dissemination have not been systematically reexamined. Consequently, two-century old concepts about fairy tales live on in folklore as well as in related fields such as literature, history, and psychology.

For the time being, globalization has made nationalistic agendas irrelevant for fairy tale scholars and their institutional supporters. This may offer hope that evidence for fairy tale origins among urban folk and fairy tales' original production by and for urban folk will be taken sufficiently seriously so that people will begin to question the old myths.

Library shelves, however, continue to be dominated by the conclusions reached by six generations of oralist-privileging fairy and folk tale scholars. Those conclusions do not gather dust. They remain front and center, because they provide literary scholars, historians, and the general public with "facts" on which to base their own thinking about fairy tales. The result is that in books about fairy tales, readers are typically informed that young women "told" Straparola the stories of *Pleasant Nights*, that Basile "wrote down" the *Pentamerone* stories recounted by a passel of common women, that nursemaids provided late seventeenth-century French fairy tale authors with the stories they similarly "wrote down," and that the Grimms "recorded" tales from the German folk. The result is a country otherness about fairy tales that contradicts their sixteenth- and seventeenth-century urban creation and their twentieth-century urban consumption.

The basic argument of this book replaces an anonymous folk with literate authors who are city-oriented people like ourselves. For human mouths and ears it substitutes printed books as the route of dissemination. This argument has an ancestry. In 1867 a young doctoral candidate at the University of Göttingen, F. J. W. Brakelman, argued that Straparola's stories underlay many of the Grimms' tales. A generation later, as national folklore societies were being founded in the late 1880s, a vigorous debate between oralists and non-oralists took place in Germany, France, England, and the United States. Without exception oralists won the day. After yet another generation, in the 1920s and early 1930s, an Austrian-born Czech named Albert Wesselski argued for a top-down history of the dissemination of fairy tales. He replaced the idea of folk oral creation and transmission with a concept of literate creation and textual transmission. But Nazi Germany with its taste for *völkisch*-ness was no place to advance a non-folk-based and hence dangerously heretical idea. Wesselski's position was ridiculed for the next seventy years, with "Wesselski redivivus" still considered a mortal critical thrust.

Many contemporaries are exploring alternative ways to understand the oral qualities that form part and parcel of authored fairy tales. Rudolf Schenda brought his years of study of oral narrative together in *Von Mund zu Ohr* (From Mouth to Ear, 1993). Few of his writings are available in English, but a key section of his lengthy disquisition on the nature of orality was finally published in 2007.[12] Taking a different tack, an English literature critic, Susan Stewart adopted the prevailing view of fairy tales' orality in her 1991 *Crimes of Writing: Problems in the Containment of Representation* and categorized them as a "distressed" genre. She was using the furniture finishing term "distressed," the practice of beating a newly manufactured piece with clubs or chains until it develops an aged appearance. Even though her adherence to oral origins is, I believe, invalid, her term "distresesed" captures well the process to which fairy tales have been subjected by modern commentators, either because they genuinely thought that fairy tales were an ancient literary artifact from the childhood of humanity or because they meant to give the impression that that was so. Elizabeth Harries shares Susan Stewart's vision of fairy tales as a genre whose producers have built agedness into their creations, but for Harries the "*imitations* of what various literary cultures have posited as the traditional, the authentic, or the nonliterary" provide a starting point for analyzing the means by which authors have aged the tales they composed.[13] Diane Dugaw examined ballads in the context of cheap print and came to the conclusion that "[t]he longstanding insistence upon the orality of folk tradition is a political idea whose oversimplifications have been in most cases misleading at best."[14] Her findings and her conclusions about ballads parallel those I've come to about fairy tales and suggest that the time has come for a wholesale reconsideration of orality as the inevitable means by which European fairy tales spread throughout the world. The slowly-emerging evidence from printing and publishing history provides an explanation that is substantial, verifiable, and superior to two centuries of largely conjectural theories about oral transmission.

Above all, a book-based history of fairy tales shows that fairy tales emerged when cities, literate city people, and city possibilities intersected and became a reality in urban people's lives. Venice was the first place where large-scale commerce, manufacturing, wide-spread literacy, and cheap print existed in the same place at the same time. Each of these conditions was a necessary element in the mix needed to produce fairy tales as we know them in the modern world. And so it can be no surprise that it was in Venice where, for the first time, the beloved plot of modern rags-to-riches-through-magic-and-marriage fairy tales sprang into existence and joined the old restoration plots that had long entertained Europe's tale lovers. Rise fairy tales were new stories for a new age. They were stories about people like us.

NOTES

1. WHY A NEW HISTORY OF FAIRY TALES?

1. For more on definitions and discussions of folktales vs. fairy tales see Bottigheimer, "Fairy Tales and Folktales" (1996), "Fairy Tales" (1999), "Germany" (2000), *Fairy Godfather* (2002), "Märchen, Märchenliteratur" (2002), "Folk and Fairy Tales" (2003), "The Ultimate Fairy Tale" (2003), and "Fairy Tale Origins, Fairy Tale Dissemination, and Folk Narrative Theory" (2006).
2. Bottigheimer, "Luftschlösser," *Enzyklopädie des Märchens* 8 (1996): cols. 1260–1265.
3. For analyses of these tales, see Bottigheimer, *Grimms' Bad Girls and Bold Boys* (1987).
4. See Bottigheimer, *Fairy Godfather* (2002) 11–13 for an extended discussion of restoration fairy tales.
5. Ibid., 13–18 for an extended discussion of rise fairy tales.
6. See Briggs, *Encyclopedia of Fairies* (1976) and *The Vanishing People* (1978). Reginald Scot referred familiarly to scores of different kinds of extranatural figures in his *Discouerie of Witchcraft* (1584); Bottigheimer, "Misperceived Perceptions about Perrault's Fairy Tales and the History of English Children's Literature" (2002) 3.
7. Bottigheimer, "'An Important System of Its Own': Defining Children's Literature" (1998) 195–196.

8. Duval, *Littérature de colportage et imaginire collectif en Angleterre à l'époque des Dicey (1720–v.1800)* (1991).

9. For detailed discussions of distinctions between tales about fairyland and fairy tales, see Bottigheimer "Fairy Tales and Folktales" (1996), "Fairy Tales" (1999), "Märchen, Märchenliteratur" (2002), and "Folk and Fairy Tales" (2003).

10. Ben Jonson, *The Entertainment at Althorpe* (1604); "R. S." *A Description of the King and Queene of Fayries, their habit, fare, their abode, pompe, and state* (1635).

11. Delattre, *English Fairy Poetry* (1912) 191.

12. Irving took his story from "Peter Klaus" in Otmar's (that is, J. K. C. Nachtigall's) *Volcks-Sagen* of 1800. See Bottigheimer, "Irving, Washington" (1993).

13. J. R. R. Tolkien discussed tales about fairies and fairyland extensively in an essay, "On Fairy-Stories," in his 1964 book *Tree and Leaf*. He recognized that fairy tales like ones in collections by Perrault, the Grimms, and Andrew Lang differ profoundly from "fairy-stories," i.e. tales about fairies and fairyland. Nonetheless, he applied the term fairy-story. His project was to sort tales about fairies and fairyland out from all of the other kinds of tales people carelessly called fairy-stories, such as beast fables and Lewis Carroll's *Alice* stories. He found fairy-stories "very ancient indeed" (24). Ultimately he returned to "faërie" as a necessary component in fairy-stories, but like others who wrote before and after he did, Tolkien ended up conflating *Märchen* with folktales, fairy-stories, nursery-tales, and by implication, fairy tales ("On Fairy Tales" 17–18, 24, 26).

14. Cited from *Perrault. Contes*, ed. Rouger (1967) xxii. See also Mme de Sévigné, *Lettres de Mme Sévigné* (1992).

15. This confusion exists far less in Italian literary history than in English, French, and German, because historically there has been less Italian literary interest in tales about fairyland, even though an ample amount of Arthurian material made itself at home in late medieval and early modern Italian romances.

16. Brian Pullan, *Rich and Poor in Renaissance Venice: The Social Institutions of a Catholic State to 1620* (1971); ibid., "Town Poor, Country Poor: The Province of Bergamo from the Sixteenth to the Eighteenth Century" (1999).

17. See, for instance, Perrault's folktale rendering of "The Three Ridiculous Wishes," or the Grimms' "Hans in Luck" or "Clever Elsie."

18. Bottigheimer, "Straparola's *Piacevoli Notti*: Rags-to-Riches Fairy Tales as Urban Creations" (1994).

19. Grendler, *Schooling in Renaissance Italy* (1989).

20. Burke, *The Italian Renaissance: Culture and Society in Italy* (1987) 111; Grendler, *Schooling in Renaissance Italy* (1989); ibid., "What Piero Learned in School" (1995); Santagiuliana, *Caravaggio: Profilo storico* (1981) 100; Bottigheimer, *Fairy Godfather* (2002) 49–50.

21. Moser-Rath, *Dem Kirchvolk die Leviten gelesen* ... (1991); Berlioz, Brémond, Velay-Vallantin, eds., *Formes Médiévales du conte merveilleux* (1989).

22. Merchants often had their newly purchased books bound in richly tooled leather, while artisans typically stitched together the folded sheets of a newly bought "book" themselves in a strong but crude binding.

23. Bottigheimer, "Straparola's *Piacevoli Notti*: Rags-to-Riches Fairy Tales as Urban Creations." (1994) 281–296.

24. Rapp, *Industry and Economic Decline in Seventeenth-Century Venice* (1976).

25. Chojnacki, *Women and Men in Renaissance Venice* (2000) 53–75.

26. Bottigheimer, chapter 1, "Restoration and Rise" in *Fairy Godfather* (2002).

27. Wilson, *The World in Venice: Print, The City, and Modern Identity* (2004); Quondam, "Mercanzia d'honore, mercanzia d'utile: produzione libraria e lavoro intellectuale a Venezia nel '500" (1977).

28. Bottigheimer, "France's First Fairy Tales" (2005).

29. Grätz, *Das Märchen in der deutschen Aufklärung* (1988).

30. Tomkowiak, "Traditionelle Erzählstsoffe im Lesebuch" (1989); Bottigheimer, "Luckless, Witless, and Filthy-footed" (1993) 259–284.

31. Bottigheimer, "Luckless, Witless, and Filthy-footed" (1993) provides one such continuous publishing history from 1550s Venice to Europe's overseas empires.

32. Bottigheimer, *Fairy Godfather* (2002) 45–58, 13–18.

33. In the "Introduction" to *The Oxford Companion to Fairy Tales*, Jack Zipes assigns the term "oral wonder tale" to a purportedly pre-1500s "literary fairy tale." In his version of fairy tale history "oral

wonder tales," the product of the folk, have existed for "thousands of years" and are the basis for tales that were appropriated and written down by men such as Straparola, Basile, and Perrault "to serve the hegemonic interest of males within the upper classes of particular communities and societies . . ." (xx).

34. Zipes, for instance, enunciates the theory of orality in the introduction to his textbook *The Great Fairy Tale Tradition* in the following terms: "In fact, the literary fairy tale has evolved from the stories of the oral tradition, piece by piece in a process of incremental adaptation, generation by generation in the different cultures of the people who cross-fertilized the oral tales and disseminated them" (xi).

35. In *Histoire d'un conte* (1985), a broad study of "Puss in Boots," Denise Escarpit emphasizes Perrault's tale although she acknowledges that he may have used Straparola's (1553) and Basile's (1634) earlier versions as sources. For an analysis showing the extent of Perrault's indebtedness to Straparola see Bottigheimer, *Fairy Godfather* (2002) 125–128.

36. Bottigheimer, "France's First Fairy Tales" (2005).

37. See Blamires, "The Early Reception of the Grimms' *Kinder- und Hausmärchen* in England" (1989); Sutton, *The Sin-Complex* (1996), and Schacker, *National Dreams* (2003).

38. The stability of popular stories published and read over centuries is laid out in Schenda's *Volk ohne Buch* (1970) and *Die Lesestoffe der Kleinen Leute* (1976).

2. TWO ACCOUNTS OF THE GRIMMS' TALES

1. Rölleke in Grimm (1980) 3:572–573.

2. Ibid., 3:454. The notation itself can be seen in a photomechanical reproduction in Grimm, (1812); rpt. (1986) 1:122.

3. Ibid., 3:562. Jacob also recorded "Rapunzel" (No. 12). Although he didn't indicate its origins, it was for a long time attributed to a female informant. Its origins lay in a book by Friedrich Schulz.

4. For additional information about Friederike Mannel see Paradiž, *Clever Maids* (2005) 58–66; Rölleke in Grimm (1980) 3: 567;

Hennig and Lauer, *200 Jahre Brüder Grimm* (1985) 538. The Ramus sisters contributed a single but very important tale, No. 9 "The Twelve Brothers" (Rölleke in Grimm, (1980) 3: 368).

5. For a nuanced and accurate account of Frau Viehmann's role, see Hennig and Lauer, 545–546.

6. Rölleke in Grimm (1980) 3: 560, 563–565.

7. Quoted by Seitz, *Die Brüder Grimm: Leben* (1984) 70.

8. Rölleke in Grimm (1980) 3:566; Hettinga, *The Brothers Grimm* (2001) 72.

9. It is easy to validate this statement by examining the listings of informants and the tales they provided. Rölleke has made this readily accessible in "Beiträger und Vermittler der Märchen" in Grimm (1980) 3:559–574.

10. My translation, "Vorrede" in (1812) *Kinder- und Hausmärchen* 1: v–xxi, here, 1:v, from Rölleke in Grimm (1986).

11. Ibid., 1:vii.

12. ". . . where we are from" (ibid.).

13. It is obvious that Wilhelm was here referring not to the girls and young women whom he knew, but to those whom he firmly believed were the oral sources behind the Wild, Hassenpflug, Ramus, and Mannel girls' tales, because he asserted that they "are steadily becoming fewer in number" (ibid.).

14. Ibid.

15. Ibid.

16. Ibid., 1:viii–ix.

17. In the first edition, Wilhelm footnoted the text at this point: "This relationship occurs often and is probably the first cloud that rises on a child's clear blue sky and that squeezes out the first tears unseen by people but counted by the angels. Even flowers take their names from this situation, the *viola tricolor* is called "Little Stepmother," because each of the yellow petals has a tiny narrow green petal underneath, which the mother gave her own cheerful children; the two stepchildren stand above, mourning in dark purple and have no place to sit." (Grimm (1812); rpt. (1986) 1: ix).

18. Ibid., 1:ix–x.

19. Ibid., 1:xviii.

20. Ibid., 1:xiii.

21. Ibid., 1:xiv.

22. Well-known scholars from the past who have put oral composition and transmission in the center of their research and results include, but are not limited to, Walter Anderson, Linda Dégh, Bengt Holbek, Carl Wilhelm Sydow, and Alan Dundes. Prominent "laws" and theories of folk narrative include Anderson's "Law of Self- Correction," Laurits Bødker's "Tradition Bearer Theory," Linda Dégh and A. Vázsonyi's "Conduit Theory," the varying polygenesis theories of the Grimms, Theodor Benfey, Gaston Paris, Emmanuel Cosquin, Joseph Bédier, Andrew Lang, and the Krohns, father and son, as well as various concepts of pure oral vs. contaminated literary tale variants. For a treatment of this subject, see Bottigheimer, "Fairy Tale Origins, Fairy Tale Dissemination, and Folk Narrative Theory" (2006).

23. In the *Zeugnisse* (Evidence) section of the lengthy appendix to the *Kinder- und Hausmärchen* published towards the end of their scholarly careers in 1856, the Grimms repeatedly imply an existence of *Märchen* in the sense of modern fairy tales in the medieval period. However, in the forty years that had passed since they had first confidently asserted this in the foreword to the First Edition, they were still unable to cite a single one. See Rölleke in Grimm (1980) 271–414 [=285–426].

24. "One more highly notable circumstance is explained by the ubiquity of tales, namely the broad diffusion of these German tales. They have not only spread as far as the heroic legends ("Heldensagen") of Siegfried the Dragon Slayer, but they even exceed them in extent, considering that we find them spread throughout all of Europe, with the result that a relationship among the noblest peoples reveals itself" (ibid., 1:xiv–xv).

25. 1815; rpt.1986 2:iv–v.

26. Ibid., 2:v.

27. Ibid., 2:v–vi.

28. Ibid., 2:vi.

29. Ibid.

30. Ibid., 2:vii–viii.

31. Ibid., 2:viii–ix.

32. Ibid., 2:ix.

33. Ibid., 2:x.

34. Ibid., 2:x; "Alles aber, was aus mündlicher Ueberlieferung hier gesammelt worden, ist sowohl nach seiner Entstehung als Ausbildung (vielleicht darin den gestiefelten Kater allein ausgenommen) rein deutsch und nirgends her erborgt, wie sich, wo man es in einzelnen Fällen bestreiten wollte, leicht auch äusserlich beweisen liesse" (Ibid., 2:xi).

35. Bottigheimer, "The Publishing History of Grimms' Tales" (1993) 79.

36. First Edition (1815); rpt. (1986) 2: xi. Wilhelm withdrew this content entirely from the preface to the Second Edition. He and his brother Jacob could read many languages, including French, and they used their knowledge to construct some of their tales. See for example, the clear similarities in the succession of events and the content of conversations in the Perrault "Red Riding Hood" tale and the Grimms' first versions as reproduced in Lauer, *Dorothea Viehmann und die Brüder Grimm* (1997) 85–88.

37. See Musäus, "Vorbericht an Herrn David Runkel, Denker und Küster an der St. Sebalds-Kirche in ***" in *Volksmährchen der Deutschen* ([1782] 1868) xi–xvi.

38. Tomkowiak, "Traditionelle Erzählstoffe im Lesebuch. Ein Projekt zur schulischen Geschichtspädagogik zwischen 1770 und 1920" (1989).

39. Ellis famously outlined disparities between the Grimms' (and many scholars') claims about unchanged texts in *One Fairy Story Too Many* (1983).

40. As falsely pictured by L. Katzenstein c. 1894. See reproduction in Lauer (1997) 353 and in Seitz (1984) 62.

41. "Fairy Tales about Fairy Tales: Notes on Canon Formation" is the title of chapter 1 in Harries, *Twice Upon a Time: Women Writers and the History of the Fairy Tale* (2001).

42. As Harder has demonstrated in "die Marburger Frühromantik" (1996), Marburg was a center for German Early Romanticism at precisely the time of the Grimms' study there. Through Savigny they imbibed the powerful spirit of Jena Romanticism as well as becoming aware of, and being made known to, Romantic thought as

exemplified most famously by Clemens Brentano and the von Arnim family, and the Grimms' early work and understanding of history and literature grew naturally from these beginnings.

43. This is well documented in Grätz, *Das Märchen in der deutschen Aufklärung* (1988).

44. With pay that was considerably lower than Jacob's had been under Jérôme.

45. Seitz 62.

46. *Achim von Arnim und Jacob und Wilhelm Grimm* (1904) 271.

47. Dortchen was his mother Dorothea Wild (born 1793); Gretchen and Lisette were her older sisters, Herman's aunts, Margareta (born 1787) and Elisabeth (born 1782). Jeanette and Male were Johanna (born 1791) and Amalia Hassenpflug (born 1800). Mie has been identified as Wilhelmine von Schwertzell (born 1790), but it is more likely to have been Dorothea Wild's own sister Mie Wild (Rölleke, "'Old Marie': The End of a Myth" [1986] 289–290).

48. Cited in Rölleke (1986) 290, but originally published by Herman Grimm in *Deutsche Rundschau* (1895) 97.

49. Rölleke (1986) 292.

50. Ibid., 296.

51. A textual comparison by de Blécourt in "On the Origin of 'Hänsel and Gretel'" indicates that Dortchen Grimm had read the 1801 *Feenmarchen*.

52. This is abundantly clear from Grätz, *Das Märchen in der deutschen Aufklärung* (1988).

53. See their lengthy footnote in Volume 1 of the First Edition (1812); rpt. (1986) 1: xix–xx.

54. Hassenpflug tales that had passed through French channels include "The White Snake" (No. 17), "Sleeping Beauty" (No. 50), "The Water Nixie" (No. 79), and "The Golden Key" (No. 200). Friederike Mannel provided "Fundevogel" (No. 51), and "Die Goldkinder" (No. 85). The Wild family may have contributed "The Frog Prince" (No. 1), young Dortchen was responsible for "The Singing Bones" (No. 28), "Die Wichtelmänner" (No. 39), "The Six Swans" (No. 49), "Der liebste Roland" (No. 56), and "Many Furs" (No. 65), while her sister Gretchen provided "Mary's Child" (No. 3).

3. THE LATE SEVENTEENTH- AND EIGHTEENTH-CENTURY LAYERS

1. Nineteenth-century scholars often claimed outright that late seventeenth- and early eighteenth-century French fairy tale authors had taken their tales from the folk. Twentieth- and twenty-first-century scholars more often than not use language that is consistent with that premise and describe people like Mme d'Aulnoy, Charles Perrault, and others as "writing down" tales that they "heard."

2. This represents in shorthand form the three waves propounded by Grätz in *Das Märchen in der deutschen Aufklärung. Vom Feenmärchen zum Volksmärchen*. For a list of fairy tale books published in Germany in the eighteenth century, see Grätz, Anhang (331–397).

3. The title continues: *Aus dem französischen übersetzt. Mit einer Vorrede (Friedr[ich] Eberh[ard] Rambachs)* (Halle: Gebauer, 1758).

4. See listings of publications under varying titles in Brüggemann and Ewers, *Handbuch zur Kinder- und Jugendliteratur. Von 1750 bis 1800* (1982) cols. 1426–1429.

5. Also eventually into Spanish (1846).

6. Less known among fairy tale scholars is the fact that her book alternated stories from the Bible with edited and moralized fairy tales from earlier French authors.

7. Looking at her tellings of French fairy tales, we realize that it was more often than not in Mme Leprince de Beaumont's version that such fairy tales came out in popular press *Bibliothèque bleue* chapbooks.

8. Brüggemann and Ewers (1982) 75–77.

9. Bottigheimer, "Before *Contes du temps passe* (1697): 'Grisélidis. Nouvelle' (1691), 'Souhaits ridicules. Conte' (1693), and 'Peau d'Asne. Conte' (1694)" (forthcoming); ibid., "Perrault au travail" (2007).

10. ". . . la couleur du Temps." "Temps" is usually translated as "the sky" or "the heavens," but could just as well be translated as "weather" or "time," either of which represents a far more impossible task than procuring a skyblue gown.

11. Murat, *Histoires sublimes et allégoriques* (1699) "Avertissement" n.p.

12. Interestingly, one of Basile's other stories has an ass-skin-clad figure—a witch who wrapped herself in an ass's skin to keep lions at bay ("Petrosinella," Day 2, Story 1).

13. Magnanini, "Postulated Routes from Naples to Paris: The Printer Antonio Bulifon and Giambattista Basile's Fairy Tales in Seventeenth-Century France" (2007): 78–92.

14. Francillon (1995); Raynard (2007).

15. Wolfzettel indicates that Mlle Lhéritier's dependence on Basile was likely, but avoids asserting it as a fact, which I wish to do here. See Wolfzettel (1996).

16. Mlle Lhéritier had completed her MS. by 19 June 1695, when it was granted its privilege. The book was registered on 18 August 1695, and its printing had been completed by 8 October 1695.

17. Published in *La tour ténebreuse* (1705).

18. Basile's tale of disguise was "Le tre corone" (The Three Crowns, Day 4, Story 6).

19. *Mlle Lhéritier . . . Contes*, ed. Robert (2005) 48–49.

20. ". . . contes impertinents"; "grossièretés d'un certain caractère" (*Mlle Lhéritier . . . Contes*, ed. Robert (2005) 51).

21. Ibid. 54, 56.

22. Although the *Oeuvres Meslees* in which "Marmoisan" appears bears the imprint date 1696, it received its privilege in September 1695 and was thus written before that date.

23. The reverse argument could also be made, namely, that Mlle Lhéritier copied from Perrault. However, Perrault's record of reworkings far exceeds Lhéritier's.

24. In the N. M. Penzer translation.

25. The fact that the girls behind the forbidden door are in the bloom of health, rather than hanging, bloody, from the rafters, as Perrault has it, casts new light on his creation of the "Bluebeard" morality tale.

26. Basile (trans. and ed. Canepa) (2007) 9.

27. Basile (ed. Michele Rak) (1986) 760.

28. Ibid., 761.

29. According to Schenda, *Folklore e Letteratura* (1986) 3.

30. Bottigheimer, "France's First Fairy Tales" (2005).

31. In Basile's "Peruonto" the ugly hero "was transformed from a fly-catcher into a goldfinch, from an ogre into a Narcissus, from a grotesque mask into a lovely little doll." (Basile [trans. Canepa] (2007) 68) We may disregard the Narcissus and the doll, but it is precisely a little bird into which Mme d'Aulnoy has her homely hero change himself to gain access to his beloved princess at night in Madame d'Aulnoy, "Le Dauphin. Conte" in *Contes des Fées* (2004) 1007–1037.

32. For example, in its paternity trial, princely lunacy, and execution-ary barrel for the little family.

33. This simple statement glosses over a current debate about whether Perrault or contemporary women writers were the first to write fairy tales. Defining Mme d'Aulnoy's "Ile de la Félicité" as a fairy tale has caused this problem. It is, however, manifestly a tale about fairyland rather than as a fairy tale (see chapter 1, 8–17). If this distinction is recognized, then it appears that Charles Perrault and Mlle Lhéritier were the first French authors to write fairy tales in France, not Mme d'Aulnoy. Another instance of Mme d'Aulnoy's having drawn on Perrault can be found in "La Chatte Blanche," in whose palace cat portraits hang. Her Puss in Boots portrait is neither that of Stra-parola's nor of Basile's cat, but of Perrault's, that is, the "Chat botté, marquis de Carabas" (Aulnoy [1698; rpt. (2004)] 758).

34. Perrault's good stepsister derives her virtue from her father, her vice from her mother, which is the case with Lhéritier's girls and implicitly the same in Basile (3,10). Perrault's good girl is rewarded with flowers (Basile 4,7) and jewels (Lhéritier) from her mouth; Perrault's bad sister suffers from serpents and toads from her mouth (to which Lhéritier added spiders, mice, and vile creatures). Fur-thermore, Perrault's prince likes the idea of a jewel-producing wife, just as Basile did (4,7). On the other hand, Lhéritier concludes her tale with an italicized quotation from Perrault, identifying the lo-cation of the bad sister's death as *"au coin d'un boisson"* (90); Per-rault had similarly had her die "au coin d'un buisson" in his 1695 MS, but changed the wording for the print version in 1697 to *"au coin d'un bois"* (rpt. (1980) [ed. Barchilon] 115).

4. THE TWO INVENTORS OF FAIRY TALE TRADITION

1. In Lewis Seifert's discussion of fairy tale magic and the way in which it functioned in Baroque (here French) poetics, *vraisemblance* is equivalent to "verisimilitude" and / or "plausibility" (26, 232n10). Although Seifert's discussion concerns seventeenth-century France, a concern for the likelihood that a plot could have developed in the way that it was presented was one that also imbued the earlier Italian novella tradition, including those that formed part of secular tale collections. See Seifert, *Fairy Tales, sexuality and gender in France 1690–1715* (1996), Chapter 1, "Marvelous realities" (esp. 26–36).

2. Chaucer's *Canterbury Tales* is unusual in siting its narratives on a journey without threatening dangers and in having storytellers who represent a cross section of medieval society.

3. In particular Boccaccio used tales from the *Golden Ass* of Apuleius, the *Disciplina clericalis* of Petrus Alphonsi, stories from *Barlaam and Josaphat*, the *Novellino*, the *Speculum historiale* of Vincent of Beauvais, and the *Comoedia Lydiae* of Matthew of Vendome. See Spinette (1979) 2: 550.

4. There was one exception, and that was the concluding story of the collection, "Griselda," which existed nowhere before Boccaccio composed it, although there had been plenty of tales of suffering womanhood from antiquity through the entire middle ages.

5. Boccaccio (1352) (trans. Payne; rpt. (1982)) 1:3.

6. The first story of the first day set the tone that would be followed throughout: "It is a seemly thing, dearest ladies, that whatsoever a man does, he give it beginning from the holy and admirable name of Him who was the maker of all things. Wherefore, it behooving me, as the first, to begin our storytelling, I propose to begin with one of His marvels, to the end that, this being heard, our hope in Him, as in a thing immutable, may be confirmed and His name be ever praised by us" (Boccaccio (1352) (trans. Payne; rpt. (1982)) 1:27).

7. Opening statement of the *Pentamerone* frame story (Basile [trans. Canepa] (2007) 35). In its original Neapolitan it reads as follows: "Fu proverbeio de chille stascioniate, de la maglia antica, che chi cerca chello che non deve trova chello che non vole . . ." in Basile (ed. Rak) (1988) 10.

8. *Pentamerone* frame story in Basile (trans. and ed. Penzer) (1932); rpt. (1979) 1:9; Neapolitan "marmaglia" (Basile [ed. Rak] (1988) 22).

9. From Basile (trans. Canepa) (2007) 42; "Zeza scioffata, Cecca storta, Meneca vozzolosa, Tolla nasuta, Popa scartellata, Antonella vavosa, Ciulla mossuta, Paola sgargiata, Giommetella zellosa e Iacova squasquarata" in Basile (ed. Rak) (1988) 22.

10. Frame tale, Basile (trans. Canepa) (2007) 42; "fornuto de gliottere" in Basile (ed. Rak) (1988) 24.

11. Cited from Penzer's translation of Benedetto Croce's discussion of Basile's style in Basile (trans. Penzer) (1932) 1:xlix–l. Basile's sunrise and sunset metaphors are much commented upon in Basile criticism.

12. Battista Guarini (1538–1612), *Il Pastor fido* as cited in Schenda Afterword in Basile (trans. Schenda et al.) (2000) 494–495.

13. Ibid., 495.

14. My thanks to Suzanne Magnanini for explaining Basile's and his contemporaries' understanding of the marvelous.

15. Baroque literary magic forms part of a complex discussion of the marvelous and inducing a condition of marvelling among readers, which lies beyond the scope of this brief discussion of the history of fairy tales.

16. For a modern explication of Italian academies with reference to fairy tales, see Suzanne Magnanini, "Telling Tales Out of School: The Fairy Tale and Italian Academies" forthcoming.

17. Basile (trans. Penzer) (1932) 1:xviii.

18. Minieri Riccio, "Accademie fiorite in Napoli," *Archivio storico per le province napoletane* 5.3 (luglio-settembre 1880) 148–149. Riccio names Oziosi members who included the Viceroy, Count of Lemnos, Italian and Spanish scholars and men of letters, as well as many great nobles. See also Magnanini as note 16 above; Girolamo De Miranda *Una quiete operosa* (2000) for detailed descriptions of meetings of literary academies; Otis H. Green, "The Literary Court of the Conde de Lemos at Naples. 1610–1616" 1 (1933) 290–308. My grateful thanks to Suzanne Magnanini for guidance into the world of Italian academies.

19. Rak in Basile, ed. Rak (1988) xxxii–xxxv.

20. In Basile's "The Cockroach, The Mouse, and The Cricket" (Day 3, Story 5), a German prince suffering from cockroach-induced

diarrhea on his wedding night provides low comedy, whose Rabelaisian humor can only be dignified and legitimated by Bakhtinian reasoning.

21. Basile (trans. Canepa) (2007) 168.
22. Ibid., 344.
23. Ibid., 168.
24. Ibid., 416; "Talia, che vedde le cose male arriate 'ngenocchiatase 'nante ad essa la pregaie c'a lo manco le desse tanto tiempo che se spogliasse li vestite c'aveva n'cuollo" (Basile [ed. Rak] (1988) 950.
25. Basile (trans. Canepa) (2007) 83; "Zezolla, 'nmezzata da la maiestra ad accidere la matrela e credenno co farele avere lo patre pe marito d'essere tenuta cara, è posta a la cucina; ma, pe vertute de le fate, dapò varie fortune se guadagna no re pe marito" (Basile (ed. Rak) (1988) 124).
26. Basile (trans. Canepa) (2007) 84; Basile (ed. Rak) (1988) 124, 126.
27. Basile (trans. Canepa) (2007) 84; Basile (ed. Rak) (1988) 126.
28. Basile (trans. Canepa) (2007) 87; Basile (ed. Rak) (1988) 134.
29. For an analysis of the Italian origins and the worldwide spread of this fascinating tale, see Bottigheimer, "Luckless, Witless, and Filthy-Footed" (1993).
30. For a historical corrective to the historically error-filled account that Straparola provided, see Bottigheimer, Fairy Godfather (2002) 91–103.
31. In a two-fold restoration fairy tale, Princess Doralice escaped her lustful father Tebaldo and married a king, but her father pursued her, murdered her children, and inculpated his daughter. Condemned to a slow and miserable death by burial up to her armpits, Doralice was saved by the arrival of her childhood nursemaid, who recounted her sad history and accused her father, who was tortured and executed. Released and restored to health, Doralice and her husband had more children and lived happily ever after.
32. Prince Livoretto of Tunis left home to seek his fortune, and worked at humble jobs until being sent by the Sultan of Cairo to fetch Princess Bellisandra of Damascus. Having fallen in love with her escort, Bellisandra used magic skills to persuade her husband to let her cut off his head, after which she and Livoretto married and lived happily ever after. Prince Guerrino of Sicily,

forced to flee his father's wrath for having freed a prize prisoner, is supplied with a magic horse and money by his mother and is helped by a mysterious youth to marriage with the beautiful Potentiana and eventually to inheriting kingship in the kingdom of his birth.

33. In "Prince Pig" (Night 2, Story 1) three impoverished sisters are married to a prince who's been enchanted into the shape and manners of a pig. He kills the first two, but the third, who embraces her fate and her swinish husband, survives, helps disenchant him, and lives happily ever after.

34. This was Costantino Fortunato, the hero of Straparola's "Puss in Boots" tale (Night 11, Story 1).

35. As did Dionigi, apprentice to the sorcerer Lattantio (Night 8, Story 4).

36. See note 33 above.

37. Adamantina and her sister Cassandra inherited only a chest of linen fluff, but their fortune changed when an old woman gave Adamantina a doll that rewarded her love by defecating gold coins. The doll, stolen by a covetous neighbor, was thrown onto a rubbish heap, where a king found it when he looked for something with which to wipe himself after a fit a diarrhea. Incensed, the doll bit into his nether parts most painfully and remained there until the king promised to marry whoever freed him from his torment. Adamantina did so, was rewarded with a royal wedding, and lived happily ever after.

38. The lazy Dionigi couldn't learn tailoring from Master Lattantio, for which he was daily beaten, but he studied his master's practices of necromancy and used them to woo a princess. The tale culminates with dramatic shapeshifting, as the sorcerer (as a rooster) tries to destroy Dionigi by pecking up all the pomegranate seeds into which he's changed himself. Dionigi prevails, marries the princess, his father becomes rich, and everyone lives happily ever after.

39. Schenda, "Semi-Literate and Semi-Oral Processes," (2007) 127–140.

40. Bin Gorion, ed. *Mimekor Yisrael* (1990) 70–72.

41. I argue this point in detail in "*Fairy Godfather*, Fairy Tale History, and Fairy Tale Scholarship," *Journal of American Folklore* (forthcoming).

42. For the text of *Asinarius*, see Ziolkowski, *Fairy Tales from Before Fairy Tales* (2006) 341–350.

5. A NEW HISTORY

1. With reference to Dicey, see Duval (1991); with reference to d'Aulnoy see Jones, "Madame d'Aulnoy's Eighteenth-century roles as an English Lady and then as Mother Bunch" (2008).
2. Siegert, "Aufklärung und Volkslektüre" (1978).
3. See Schenda, "Semi-Literate and Semi-Oral Processes" (2007) 127–140.
4. Tomkowiak, "Traditionelle Erzählstoffe im Lesebuch" (1989); see also Tomkowiak, *Lesebuchgeschichten* (1993).
5. Bottigheimer, *Grimms' Bad Girls and Bold Boys* (1987) 21–23.
6. Trinquet, "On Literary Origins of Folkloric Fairy Tales" (2007).
7. Bottigheimer, "Bettelheims Hexe" (1989).
8. Letters or diaries in which readers of fairy tales record their taste for fairy tales would constitute direct evidence.
9. Apo, "The Relationship between Oral and Literary Tradition as a Challenge in Finnish Fairy-Tale Research" (2007) 19–33.
10. Research giving clear and indisputable evidence of the primacy of the written word at the oral-written interface was presented in talks by Brían Ó Catháin (National University of Ireland at Maynooth), Nathalie Guézennec (Paris 10, Nanterre), John Conteh-Morgan (Ohio State University), Janice Curruthers and Caroline Sumpter (both Queens University Belfast) at "The Conte: Oral and Written Interfaces," a conference held 1–2 September 2006 at Queens University Belfast.
11. Bottigheimer, "Fairy Tale Origins, Fairy Tale Dissemination, and Folk Narrative Theory" (2006) discusses Walter Anderson's "Law of Self Correction," Laurits Bødker's theory of tradition bearers, Linda Dégh and A. Vázsonyi's idea of group transmission in their conduit theory, and monogenesis vs. polygenesis. It is necessary to treat ballads separately from fairy tales. Albert Lord's (1912–1991) oral formulaic theory which well explicates ballads has been adapt-

ed and applied to many oral forms throughout the world, including an (inappropriate) application to fairy tales.

12. Schenda, "Semi-Literate and Semi-Oral Processes" (2007) 127–140.
13. Cited in Harries, *Twice Upon a Time* (2001) 4.
14. Dugaw, "Chapbook Publishing and the 'Lore' of 'the Folks'" (1995) 3.

WORKS CITED

Aarne, Antti, Stith Thompson, and Hans-Jörg Uther. 2004. *The Types of International Folktales: A Classification and Bibliography*. Helsinki: Academia Scientiarum Fennica. (=*Folklore Fellows Communications* 284).

Anderson, Walter. 1923. *Kaiser und Abt*. Helsinki: Academia Scientiarum Fennica (=*Folklore Fellows Communications* 42).

———. 1951. *Ein Volkskundliches Experiment* (=*Folklore Fellows Communications* 141).

Apo, Satu. 2007. "The Relationship between Oral and Literary Tradition as a Challenge in Finnish Fairy-Tale Research." *Marvels & Tales* 21.1: 19–33.

Arnim, Achim von. 1904. *Achim von Arnim und Jacob und Wilhelm Grimm*. Ed. Reinhold Steig. Stuttgart: Cotta.

Aulnoy, Marie Catherine Le Jumel de Barneville, Baronne d'. 1697–1699; rpt. 2004. *Madame d'Aulnoy. Contes des Fées suivis des Contes nouveaux ou Les Fées à la Mode. Édition critique*. Ed. Nadine Jasmin. Paris: Honoré Champion.

———. 1690. *Histoire d'Hipolyte, comte de Duglas*. 2 vols. Paris: Louis Sevestre.

Bargagli, Girolamo. 1572. *Dialogue on Games* (=Dialogo de' Giuochi che nelle vegghie sanesi si usano fare). Siena: Luca Bonetti.

Basile, Giambattista. 1613. "Le avventurose disavventure" in *Opere poetiche di Gio. Battista Basile*. Mantua: Aurelio & Lodovico Osanni fratelli.

——. 1634–1636; 1932; rpt. 1979. *Lo cunto de li cunti. The Pentamerone of Giambattista Basile*. Trans. and ed. Norman M. Penzer. Westport CT: Greenwood Press. 2 vols.

——. 1634–1636; 1986. *Lo cunto de li cunti*. Ed. Michele Rak. Milan: Garzanti.

——. 1634–1636; trans. 2000. *Giambattista Basile. Das Märchen der Märchen. Das Pentamerone*. Ed. and trans. Rudolf Schenda et al. Munich: C. H. Beck.

——. 1634–1636; 2007. *Giambattista Basile's The Tale of the Tales, or Entertainment for Little Ones*. Trans. and ed. Nancy Canepa. Detroit: Wayne State University Press.

Berlioz, Jacques, Claude Brémond, and Catherine Velay-Vallantin, eds. 1989. *Formes Médiévales du conte merveilleux*. Paris: Stock.

Bin Gorion, M. J., ed. 1990. *Mimekor Yisrael: Classical Jewish Folktales, Abridged Edition*. Dan Ben-Amos, annotations. Bloomington: Indiana University Press.

Blamires, David. 1989. "The Early Reception of the Grimms' *Kinder- und Hausmärchen* in England." *Bulletin of the John Rylands University Library of Manchester* 71.3: 63–77.

Blécourt, Willem de. 2008. "On the Origin of Hansel and Gretel" *Fabula* 49: 30–46.

Boccaccio, Giovanni. 1352. 1975; rpt. 1982. *Giovanni Boccaccio. Decameron. The John Payne translation revised and annotated by Charles S. Singleton*. Trans. John Payne, Ed. Charles S. Singleton. Berkeley: University of California Press. 2 volumes.

Bottigheimer, Ruth. 2008. "Before *Contes du temps passé* (1697): 'Grisélidis. Nouvelle' (1691), 'Souhaits ridicules. Conte' (1693), and 'Peau d'Asne. Conte' (1694)." *Romanic Review* 99.3 (May 2009): forthcoming.

——. 1989. "Bettelheims Hexe: Die fragwürdige Beziehung zwischen Märchen und Psychoanalyse" in *Psychotherapie—Psychosomatik— Medizinische Psychologie* 39: 294–299.

——. 2002. *Fairy Godfather: Straparola, Venice, and the Fairy Tale Tradition*. Philadelphia: University of Pennsylvania Press.

———. 2006. "Fairy Tale Origins, Fairy Tale Dissemination, and Folk Narrative Theory." *Fabula* 47.3–4: 11–21.

———. 1999. "Fairy Tales." *Encyclopedia of German Literature*. Ed. Matthew Konzett. Chicago: Fitzroy Dearborn.

———. 1996. "Fairy Tales and Folktales." *International Companion Encyclopedia of Children's Literature*. Ed. Peter Hunt. London: Routledge.

———. 2003. "Folk and Fairy Tales." *The Dictionary of Early Modern Europe*. Ed. Jonathan Dewald. New York: Charles Scribner.

———. 2005. "France's First Fairy Tales: The Rise and Restoration Narratives of 'Les Facetieuses Nuictz du Seigneur François Straparole'." *Marvels & Tales* 19.1: 17–31.

———. 2000. "Germany." *Oxford Companion to Fairy Tales*. Ed. Jack Zipes. Oxford / New York: Oxford University Press.

———. 1987. *Grimms' Bad Girls and Bold Boys: The Moral and Social Vision of the Tales*. New Haven: Yale University Press.

———. 1998. "'An Important System of Its Own': Defining Children's Literature." *Princeton University Library Chronicle* 69.2: 190–210.

———. 1993. "Irving, Washington." *Enzyklopädie des Märchens* 7: cols. 294–296.

———. 1993. "Luckless, Witless, and Filthy-footed: A Sociocultural Study and Publishing History Analysis of 'The Lazy Boy'." *Journal of American Folklore* 106.421: 259–284.

———. 1996. "Luftschlösser." *Enzyklopädie des Märchens* 8: cols. 1260–1265.

———. 2002. "Märchen, Märchenliteratur." *Lexikon Gender Studies*. Ed. Renate Kroll. Stuttgart: Metzler.

———. 2002. "Misperceived Perceptions about Perrault's Fairy Tales and the History of English Children's Literature." *Children's Literature* 20: 1–19.

———. 2007. "Perrault au travail." *Le conte en ses paroles: Le figuration de l'oralité dans le conte merveilleux du Classisme aux Lumières*. Eds Anne Defrance and Jean-François Perrin. Paris: Desjonquères. 150–159.

———. 1993. "The Publishing History of Grimms' Tales: Reception at the Cash Register." *The Reception of Grimms' Fairy Tales: Responses, Reactions, Revisions*. Ed. Donald Haase. Detroit: Wayne State University Press. 78–101.

———. 1994. "Straparola's *Piacevoli Notti*: Rags-to-Riches Fairy Tales as Urban Creations." *Marvels & Tales* 8.2: 281–296.

———. 2003. "The Ultimate Fairy Tale: Oral Transmission in a Literate World." *The Companion to the Fairy Tale*. Ed. Hilda Davidson, Anna Chaudhri. Cambridge: Boydell and Brewer.

Briggs, Katherine. 1976. *An Encyclopedia of Fairies, Hobgoblins, Brownies, Bogies, and Other Supernatural Creatures*. New York: Pantheon.

———. 1978. *The Vanishing People: Fairy Lore and Legends*. New York: Pantheon.

Brüggemann, Theodore and Hans-Heino Ewers. 1982. *Handbuch zur Kinder- und Jugendliteratur. Von 1750 bis 1800*. Stuttgart: Metzler.

Burke, Peter. 1987. *The Italian Renaissance: Culture and Society in Italy*. Princeton: Princeton University Press.

Castiglione, Baldassare. 1528; rpt. 1959. Trans. F. Simpson. *The Book of the Courtier*. New York: Unger.

Chojnacki, Stanley. 2000. *Women and Men in Renaissance Venice. Twelve Essays on Patrician Society*. Baltimore: Johns Hopkins University Press.

Davis, Robert C. 1994. *War of the Fists: Popular Culture and Public Violence in Renaissance Venice*. New York: Oxford University Press.

Dégh, Linda. 1981."Conduit-Theorie." *Enzyklopädie des Märchens* 3: cols. 124–126.

Dégh, Linda and A. Vázsonyi. 1971. "Legend and Belief." *Genre* 4: 281–304.

Delattre, Floris. 1912. *English Fairy Poetry from the Origins to the Seventeenth Century*. London: H. Froude.

De Miranda, Girolamo. 2000. *Una quiete operosa: forma e pratiche dell'Academia napoletana degli Oziosi, 1611–1645*. Naples: Fridericiana editrice universitaria.

Dugaw, Dianne. 1995. "Chapbook Publishing and the 'Lore' of 'the Folks'." *The Other Print Tradition: Essays on Chapbooks, Broadsides, and Related Ephemera*. Ed. Cathy Lynne Preston and Michael J. Preston. New York / London: Garland. 3–18.

Durand, Catherine. 1702. *Les Petits Soupers de l'année 1699, ou Aventures galantes, avec l'origine des fées*. Paris: J. Musier et J. Rolin.

Duval, Gilles. 1991. *Littérature de colportage et imaginire collectif en Angleterre à l'époque des Dicey (1720–v.1800)*. Talence: Presses Universitaires de Bordeaux.

Ellis, John M. 1983. *One Fairy Story Too Many: The Brothers Grimm and Their Tales*. Chicago / London: University of Chicago Press.

Escarpit, Denise. 1985. *Histoire d'un conte: Le chat botté en France et en Angleterre*. Paris: Didier Érudition.

Fink, Gonthier-Louis. 1966. *Naissance et apogée du conte merveilleux en Allemagne, 1740–1800*. Paris: Les Belles Lettres.

Francillon, Roger. 1995. "Une théorie de folklore à la fin du XVIIème siècle: Mlle Lhéritier." *Hören Sagen Lesen Lernen: Bausteine zu einer Geschichte der kommunikativen Kultur. Festschrift für Rudolf Schenda zum 65. Geburtstag*. Ed. Ursula Brunold-Bigler and Hermann Bausinger. Frankfurt: Peter Lang. 205–217.

Gomez, Madeleine-Angélique Poisson, Mme de. 1722. *Les journées amusantes dédiées au Roy*. Amsterdam: Par la Compagnie.

Grätz, Manfred. 1988. *Das Märchen in der deutschen Aufklärung. Vom Feenmärchen zum Volksmärchen*. Stuttgart: Metzler.

Green, Otis H. 1933. "The Literary Court of the Conde de Lemos at Naples. 1610–1616." *Hispanic Review* 1: 290–308.

Grendler, Paul E. 1989. *Schooling in Renaissance Italy: Literacy and Learning, 1300–1600*. Baltimore: Johns Hopkins Press.

———. 1995. "What Piero Learned in School: Fifteenth-Century Vernacular Education." *Piero della Francesca and His Legacy*. Ed. Marilyn Aronberg Lavin. Hanover NH: University Press of New England.

Grimm, Jacob and Wilhelm. 1857; rpt. 1980. *Kinder- und Hausmärchen*. Ed. Heinz Rölleke. 3 vols. Stuttgart: Reclam.

———. 1812/13, 1814/15; rpt. 1986. *Kinder- und Hausmärchen*. Ed. Heinz Rölleke. 2 vols. Göttingen: Vandenhoeck & Ruprecht.

Harder, Hans-Bernd. 1996. "Die Marburger Frühromantik (1800–1806)." *Jahrbuch Brüder Grimm-Gesellschaft* 6: 7–40.

Harries, Elizabeth Wanning. 2001. *Twice Upon a Time: Women Writers and the History of the Fairy Tale*. Princeton: Princeton University Press.

Hennig, Dieter and Bernhard Lauer. 1985. *200 Jahre Brüder Grimm. Die Brüder Grimm. Dokumente ihres Lebens und Wirkens*. Kassel: Weber & Weidemeyer.

Herranen, Gun. 1989. "A Big Ugly Man with a Quest for Narratives." *Studies in Oral Narrative. Studia Fennica* 33. Ed. Anna-Leena Siikala. Helsinki: Suomalaisen kirjakisuuden seura. 64–69.

Hettinga, Donald R. 2001. *The Brothers Grimm: Two Lives, One Legacy*. New York: Clarion Books.

Imbriani, Vittorio. 1875. "Il gran Basile." *Giornale napoletano* 1:23–55, 335–366; 2:194–220, 413–459.

Jones, Christine. 2008. "Madame d'Aulnoy's Eighteenth-century Roles as an English Lady and then as Mother Bunch." *Romantic Review* 99.3 (May 2009): forthcoming.

Jonson, Ben. 1604. *Particular Entertainments at Althorp*. London: n.p.

Lauer, Bernhard. 1998. "Jacob Grimm und Charles Perrault. Zum wiedereraufgefundenen Grimmschen Handexemplar von Perraults 'Contes du Temps Passé'." *Jahrbuch der Brüder-Grimm-Gesellschaft* 8:79–88.

———. 1997. *Dorothea Viehmann und die Brüder Grimm. Märchen und Wirklichkeit*. Kassel: Brüder-Grimm-Gesellschaft.

Leprince de Beaumont.1758. *Der Frau Maria le Prince de Beaumont Lehren der Tugend und Weisheit für die Jugend, Aus dem französischen übersetzt. Mit einer Vorrede Friedr[ich] Eberh[ard] Rambachs*. Halle: Gebauer.

Lhéritier de Villandon, Marie-Jeanne. 1695; rpt. 2005. *L'Œuvres Meslées* in *Le Cercle des conteuses. Mademoiselle Lhéritier, Mademoiselle Bernard, Mademoiselle de La Force, Madame Durand, Madame d'Auneuil. Contes* (=*Bibliothèque des Génies et des Fées* vol. 2). Ed. Raymonde Robert. Paris: Honoré Champion.

———. 1705; rpt. 2005. *La tour ténebreuse* in *Le Cercle des conteuses. Mademoiselle Lhéritier, Mademoiselle Bernard, Mademoiselle de La Force, Madame Durand, Madame d'Auneuil. Contes* (=Bibliothèque des Génies et des Fées vol. 2). Ed. Raymonde Robert. Paris: Honoré Champion.

Magnanini, Suzanne. 2007. "Postulated Routes from Naples to Paris: The Printer Antonio Bulifon and Giambattista Basile's Fairy Tales in Seventeenth-Century France," *Marvels & Tales* 21.1: 78–92.

———. 2008. "Telling Tales Out of School: The Fairy Tale and Italian Academies." *Romantic Review* 99.3 (May 2009): forthcoming.

Morlini, Girolamo. 1520;1983. *Novelle e favole*. Rome: Salerno.

———. 1520. *Morlini Novellae, cum gratis et privilegio cesareae majestatis et summi pontificus decennia duratura*. Naples: in aedibus Joan. Pasquet de Sallo.

————. 1520; rpt. 1955. *Hieronymi Morlini Pathenopei novellae, fabulae, comoediae.* Paris: P. Jannet.

————. 1520; rpt 1982. *Hieronymi Morlini Pathenopei novellae, fabulae, comoediae.* Millwood NJ: Kraus Reprints.

————. 1520; rpt 1983. *Novellae e favole.* Rome: Salerno.

Moser-Rath, Elfriede. 1991. *Dem Kirchvolk die Leviten gelesen . . . : Alltag im Spiegel süddeutscher Barockpredigten.* Stuttgart: Metzler.

Murat, Mme Henriette Julie de Castelnau, Comtesse de. 1699; rpt. 2006. *Histoires sublimes et allégoriques in Madame de Murat. Contes.* Ed. Geneviève Patard. (=*Bibliothèque des Génies et des Fées* vol. 3). Paris: Honoré Champion.

Musäus, Johann Karl August. 1782; rpt. 1868. *Volksmärchen der Deutschen.* Ed. Moritz Müller. Leipzig: Brockhaus.

Ocean of Story. See Somadeva.

Paradiž, Valerie. 2005. *Clever Maids. The Secret History of The Grimm Fairy Tales.* New York: Basic Books.

Penzer, Norman M. See Basile 1634–1636; rpt. 1932.

Périers, Bonaventure des. 1558. "L'aventure de Pernette" (Nouvelle CXXIX). *Nouvelles récréations et Joyeux devis.* Lyon: R. Granjon.

Perrault, Charles. 1697; rpt. 1980. *Contes de Perrault. Facsimilé de l'édition original de 1695–1697.* Geneva: Slatkine.

————. 1695; rpt. 1980. *Griselidis Nouvelle avec le conte de peau d'asne et celuy des souhaits ridicules. Quatrieme edition.* Ed. Jacques Barchilon.

————. 1967. *Perrault. Contes.* Ed. Gilbert Rouger. Paris: Garnier.

————. 1695; rpt. 1956. *Perrault's Tales of Mother Goose. The dedication manuscript of 1695 reproduced in collotype facsimile with introduction and critical text.* Ed. Jacques Barchilon. New York: Pierpont Morgan Library.

Pullan, Brian. 1971. *Rich and Poor in Renaissance Venice: The Social Institutions of a Catholic State to 1620.* Oxford: Blackwell.

————. 1999. "Town Poor, Country Poor: The Province of Bergamo from the Sixteenth to the Eighteenth Century". *Medieval and Renaissance Venice.* Ed. Ellen E. Kittell and Thomas E. Madden. Urbana: University of Illinois Press. 213–236.

Rak, Michele, ed. See Basile 1634–1636; rpt. and trans. 1986.

Rapp, Richard T. 1976. *Industry and Economic Decline in Seventeenth-Century Venice.* Cambridge: Harvard University Press.

Raynard, Sophie. 2007. "New Poetics vs. Old Print: Fairy Tales, Animal Fables, and the Gaulois Past." *Marvels & Tales* 21.1: 93–106.

Robert, Raymonde, ed. 2005. *Le Cercle des conteuses. Mademoiselle Lhériter, Mademoiselle Bernard, Mademoiselle de La Force, Madame Durand, Madame d'Auneuil. Contes.* (=Bibliotheque des Génies et des Fées vol. 2). Paris: Honoré Champion.

———. 2002. *Le conte de fées littéraire en France de la fin du XVIIᵉ à la fin du XVIIIᵉ siècle. Supplément bibliographique 1980–2000 établi par Nadine Jasmin avec la collaboration de Claire Debru.* Paris: Honoré Champion.

Rölleke, Heinz. 1986. "'Old Marie': The End of a Myth." *Fairy Tales and Society: Illusion, Allusion, and Paradigm.* Ed. Ruth B. Bottigheimer. Philadelphia: University of Pennsylvania Press. 287–300.

Rölleke, Heinz. See also Grimm.

Ruggiero, Guido. 1985. *The Boundaries of Eros: Sex, Crime, and Sexuality in Renaissance Venice.* New York: Oxford University Press

Quondam, Amedeo. 1977. "Mercanzia d'honore, mercanzia d'utile: produzione libraria e lavoro intellettuale a Venezia nel '500." *Libri, editori e pubblico nell'Europa moderna: Guida storico-critica.* Ed. Armando Letrucci. Rome: Laterza.

S., R. 1635. *A Description of the King and Queene of Fayries, Their Habits, Their Abode, Pompe, and State. Beeing very Delightfull to the Sense, and Full of Mirth.* London: Richard Harper.

Santagiuliana, Tullio. 1981. *Caravaggio: Profilo storico.* Treviglio: Signorelli.

Schacker, Jennifer. 2003. *National Dreams: The Remaking of Fairy Tales in Nineteenth-Century England.* Philadelphia: University of Pennsylvania Press.

Schenda, Rudolf. 1986. *Folklore e letteratura populare: Italia—Germania—Francia.* Trans. Maria Chiara Figliozzi and Ingeborg Walter. Rome: Istituto della Enciclopedia Italiana.

———. 1976. *Die Lesestoffe der Kleinen Leute. Studien zur populären Literatur im 19. und 20. Jahrhundert.* Munich: C. H. Beck.

———. 2007. "Semi-Literate and Semi-Oral Processes." Trans. Ruth B. Bottigheimer. *Marvels & Tales* 21.1 (2007): 127–140.

————. 1970. *Volk ohne Buch: Studien zur Sozialgeschichte der populären Lesestoffe 1770–1910*. Munich: Deutsche Taschenbuch Verlag.

————. 1993. *Vom Mund zu Ohr: Bausteine zu einer Kulturgeschichte volktümlichen Erzählens in Europa*. Göttingen: Vandenhoeck & Ruprecht.

Scot, Reginald. 1584; rpt. 1992. *Discouerie of Witchcraft*. New York: Dover.

Seifert, Lewis. 1996. *Fairy tales, sexuality and gender in France 1690–1715*. Cambridge: Cambridge University Press.

Seitz, Gabriele. 1984. *Die Brüder Grimm: Leben—Werk—Zeit*. Munich: Winkler.

Sercambi, Giovanni. 1972. *Novelle*. Ed. Giovanni Sinicropi. Bari: G. Laterza.

Sévigné, Marie de Rabutin-Chantal, marquise de. 1992. *1626–1666. Lettres de Mme Sévigné: images d'un siècle*. Paris: Scala.

Siegert, Reinhart. 1978. "Aufklärung und Volkslektüre. Exemplarisch dargestellt an Rudolph Zacharias Becker und seinem 'Noth- und Hülfsbüchlein'." Diss. Frankfurt am Main.

Somadeva. 1923; rpt. 1968. *The Ocean of Story Being C. H. Tawney's Translation of Somadeva's Kathō Sarit Sāgara (or Ocean of Streams of Story*. Trans C. H. Tawney. Intro. N. M. Penzer. 10 volumes. Delhi: Motilal Banarsidass.

Spinette, Albert. 1979. "Boccaccio, Giovanni." *Enzyklopädie des Märchens*. Berlin: de Gruyter. 2: cols. 549–561.

Stewart, Susan. 1991. *Crimes of Writing: Problems in the Containment of Representation*. New York: Oxford.

Straparola, Giovan Francesco. 1551, 1553; rpt. 1898. *The Facetious Nights of Giovanni Francesco Straparola da Caravaggio*. Ed. W. G. Waters. London: Society of Bibliophiles. 4 vols.

————. 1576; 1999. *Les nuits facétieuses*. Ed. Joël Gayraud. Paris: José Corti.

————. 1551, 1553. rpt. 2000. *Le piacevoli notti. Giovan Francesco Straparola. Le Piacevoli Notti*. Ed. Donato Pirovano. Rome: Salerno Editrice. 2 vols.

Sutton, Martin. 1996. *The Sin-Complex. A Critical Study of English Versions of the Grimms' Kinder- und Hausmärchen in the Nineteenth Century*. Cassel: Brüder Grimm-Gesellschaft.

Tolkien, J. R. R. 1964. "On Fairy-Stories." *Tree and Leaf*. London: Unwin Books. 9–70.

Tomkowiak, Ingrid. 1989. "Traditionelle Erzählstsoffe im Lesebuch. Ein Projekt zur schulischen Geschichtspädagogik zwischen 1770 und 1920." *Fabula* 30: 96–110.

———. 1993. *Lesebuchgeschichten. Erzählstoffe in Schullesebüchern, 1770–1920*. Berlin: de Gruyter.

Trinquet, Charlotte. 2007. "On Literary Origins of Folkloric Fairy Tales: A Comparison between Mme d'Aulnoy's 'Finette Cendron' and Frank Bourisaw's 'Belle Finette'." *Marvels & Tales* 21.1: 34–49.

Uther, Hans-Jörg. 2004. *The Types of International folktales: A Classification and Bibliography. Based on the System of Antti Aarne and Stith Thompson*. Helsinki: Academia Scientiarum Fennica. (=*Folklore Fellows Communications* 284). 3 vols.

Villeneuve, Gabrielle-Suzanne Barbot de. 1744. *La jeune Amériquaine et les contes marins*. The Hague: Aux dépens de la Compagnie.

Wilson, Bronwen. 2004. *The World in Venice: Print, The City, and Modern Identity*. Toronto: University of Toronto Press.

Wolfzettel, Friedrich. 1996. "Lhéritier de Villandon, Marie-Jeanne." *Enzyklopädie des Märchens*. Berlin: de Gruyter. 8: cols. 1011–1016.

Ziolkowski, Jan M. 2006. *Fairy Tales from Before Fairy Tales*. Ann Arbor: University of Michigan Press.

Zipes, Jack. 2001. *The Great Fairy Tale Tradition: From Straparola and Basile to the Brothers Grimm*. New York: Norton.

———. 2000. *The Oxford Companion to Fairy Tales*. New York: Oxford University Press.

———. 2006. *Why Fairy Tales Stick*. New York: Routledge.

INDEX

Aarne-Thompson-Uther tale-type classification, 5, 8
academies, literary, 83, 99; *Accademia degli Incauti*, 83; *Accademia degli Oziosi*, 83; *Accademia degli Stravaganti*, 83
"Adamantina," 94, 131n37
"Ancilotto," 85
animal tale, 32
Apo, Satu, 108
Apollonius of Tyre, King, 60
Apuleius, Lucius, 60, 128n3
Ariosto, Ludovico, 92, 96. See also *Orlando*
Arnim, Achim von, 46, 124n42
Arsenal Library, 72
Aulnoy, Marie-Catherine d', 7, 10, 16, 55–74 *passim*, 103; in England, 103; and tales about fairies and fairyland, 16, 55–74 *passim*

Bacon, Francis, 14
Bargagli, Girolamo, 99
Basile, Giambattista, 7, 10, 13, 58,75–91; as author, 79, 81; as courtier, 83; as source, 71,72–73, 75. See also *Pentamerone*
Battle of the Ancients and the Moderns, 69
"Bear, The," 89

"Beauty and the Beast," 55
Bettelheim, Bruno, 2, 107
"Biancabella," 92
bibliothèque bleue, 103, 125n7
Bibliothèque nationale, 72
Bigolina, Giulia, 101
blind(ness), 110
Blind Strömberg, 110
"Bluebeard," 29, 54, 64, 65–66, 126n25
Boccaccio. See *Decameron*
Boiardo, Matteo, 96. See *Orlando*
book production. *See* printing and publishing
borrowed plot, 21–25 *passim*, 77, 78, 82, 84; in d'Aulnoy, 57, 70–71, 75, 127n31, 127n33; in Basile, 90; in Boccaccio, 79, 128n3; in de la Force, 71–72, 89; in Grimm, 89; in Lhéritier, 57, 62–64, 75, 90, 126n15, 127n34; in Murat, 75; in Perrault, 56, 57, 59, 68–69, 73, 75, 87, 89, 90, 112n35, 126n23, 127n34; in Straparola, 91–92
Brakelman, F. J. W., 113
Brentano, Clemens, 124n42
"Briar Rose," 38. *See also* "Sleeping Beauty"
Brunhilde, 38
Bruno, Giordano, 82
Bulifon, Antoine, 107

145

TALES DISCUSSED